ST. ANNE'S
CENTURY OF SERVICE
A Legacy of Love

"The story of St. Anne's, like so many other noble charities, is filled with chapters of God's love and compassion poured on His dedicated lay and religious who open their minds, their hearts and their all..."

(From a speech given by Sister Winifred to St. Anne's Auxiliaries and friends, October 24, 1962)

ST. ANNE'S
CENTURY OF SERVICE
A Legacy of Love

SISTER CHRISTINE BOWMAN O.S.F.

ISBN: 978-1-59777-580-9
Library of Congress Cataloging-In-Publication Data Available

Book Design by: Carolyn Wendt
Printed in the United States of America

Phoenix Books, Inc.
9465 Wilshire Boulevard, Suite 315
Beverly Hills, CA 90212

10 9 8 7 6 5 4 3 2 1

DEDICATION

This book is lovingly dedicated to all of the boards, guilds, auxiliaries, donors, volunteers, staff, leaders, Sisters, and supporters whose commitment and service have made St. Anne's the beacon of hope it is today.

Blessings,
Sister Christine, osf

CENTENNIAL
1908-2008

One hundred years is tremendously significant. In Los Angeles, it is monumental. From its inception and to the present moment, St. Anne's has been a powerful response to the Gospel call of compassion for young women who are pregnant. Yet, St. Anne's has always been able to read the signs of the times and respond to those needs with a care and compassion which is so appropriate for the present moment.

I feel honored to have had a formal relationship with St. Anne's in the past. I continue to be its supporter and will continue to sing its praises, as it takes so much of Gospel proclamation and enfleshes in the day to day life of young women and children. As an Archdiocese, we are extremely proud of the past history, the present energy, and the future developments that St. Anne's will unfold as the future comes to pass.

Rev. Msgr. Royale M. Vadakin, P.A.
Moderator of the Curia / Vicar General
Archdiocese of Los Angeles
Past member, Board of Directors, St. Anne's

The St. Anne's story offers a great cast of characters and a love story of heroic courage, filled with tragic lives transformed into happy endings. It has all the makings of a Hollywood movie! It is a tiny dream that grows to be a fabulous haven of hope for troubled teens. Dedicated Sisters and volunteers make miracles happen at St. Anne's! They really are "angels" in the City of Angels!

Joan Leslie Caldwell
Actress
Trustee, St. Anne's Foundation Board

Every time I visit St. Anne's, I am reminded how compassion, commitment, and guidance can change lives. I speak with the young women who have been given the opportunity to mature and learn how to be effective parents and independent citizens. St. Anne's is about love and empowerment.

Linda Alvarez
Anchor/Reporter CBS2 and KCAL9 News

St. Anne's is a superior model for assisting single mothers and providing opportunities—an issue that is very close to my heart.

Paul Orfalea
Kinko's Founder & Author, *Copy This*

St. Anne's is an urban oasis in the midst of the most densely populated area west of the Hudson River. St. Anne's is there for young women who have had few if any opportunities to succeed in life. The obvious love and caring provided by St. Anne's to those within their care have saved many lives. From a police officer's perspective, we at the Los Angeles Police Department's Rampart Station have witnessed this love and caring up close and personal. St. Anne's is a part of the Rampart family and Rampart is a part of St. Anne's family. As we often say "somos familia." Congratulations on your first hundred years of service and we are looking forward to the next one hundred years.

Captain John Egan
Los Angeles Police Department
Rampart Division

Thanks to the Franciscan Sisters of the Sacred Heart, who sponsor St. Anne's, and all associated with it — who treasure new life in the mothers and children entrusted there. May God's blessings continue to descend upon them.

Father Virgil Cordano, OFM
Old Mission Santa Barbara

Contents

Foreword

The idea for this book began in a Centennial Committee discussion about how we would mark St. Anne's hundredth anniversary. As the plans began to unfold, we recognized we needed a comprehensive history to share the inspiring story of St. Anne's dynamic service in the City of Angels, the challenges and successes that have touched the lives of thousands of pregnant, parenting and at-risk teenagers, their children and their families. Their stories, told by many different people who were part of St. Anne's, bring its history to life, whether they came into a haven for help or simply came to help. Collectively, their triumphs led the way to the future of St. Anne's.

I uncovered writings of those who worked with St. Anne's or who came for help in this haven of new life. I invited some of our former residents who represent various eras of the past 100 years to write their reminiscences. In places I have referred to a chronicle, which is an undated typewritten document with no known author but I believe it is authentic. I've tried to present as accurate a picture of St. Anne's as possible. Profiles throughout the book give us a glimpse of the pregnant teen at the turn of the twentieth century and how she evolved through the decades to the new millennium. I hope the book gives the reader a sense of how St. Anne's continued to modify, expand, and enhance services that contributed to the needs of these women. Because there are a lot of statistics and supporting information to the stories, I've created a Notes section that gives more details on events for those who may desire additional information.

A timeline in the back of the book chronicles some major events of world history to parallel milestones in St. Anne's illustrious history.

The Franciscan Sisters of the Sacred Heart have sponsored St. Anne's since 1941. One of the earliest guiding lights was Sister Mary Winifred Falker, a woman short in stature but a real dynamo. The narrative begins with a flashback of Sister Winifred that recounts her arrival with her companion, Sister M. Madeleine Williams, as they began their ministry in early January 1941. Sister Winifred was determined to create the finest maternity home in the country and her resolve fueled her accomplishments. During her tenure as Administrator, she supervised five ground-breaking ceremonies, including three hospital wings, a medical clinic, and an educational center. Along the way, she founded 12 volunteer guilds and auxiliaries. St. Anne's size and its extensive services led to the claim that it was the largest facility of its kind in the United States, if not the world. Despite the fact that we don't have information on how St. Anne's compared with other like facilities, we do know that St. Anne's is a survivor! While most maternity homes in the United States closed in the second half of the 20th century as the result of changes in law and societal attitudes, St. Anne's has continued and thrived as it adapted to the society and to the Southern California community.

The story of St. Anne's, like so many other noble charities, reflects the chapters of love and compassion carried out by many dedicated religious and lay women and men whose contributions still influence St. Anne's today. We hope you will be inspired by the personal stories and recollections that have captured the essence of St. Anne's Legacy of Love.

Acknowledgments

I have discovered that this book, in and of itself, is its own legacy of love! The advice and support of so many people who gave of themselves, made this endeavor possible. I am grateful to Ronald Preissman who directed us to Phoenix Books, Inc., to Michael Viner, President of Phoenix Books, Inc., for undertaking the publication of this book, and to the outstanding assistance from his staff, especially Henrietta Tiefenthaler and Sonia Fiore.

As in any research project, archival retrieval and preparation involve a lot of effort. "Many hands make light work," and a host of people lent their time and expertise to lighten my load in the research. I was given valuable assistance, particularly by Sister Kathleen Moseley, O.S.F., Archivist for the Franciscan Sisters of the Sacred Heart, Frankfort, Illinois; and from all those from St. Anne's who supported the project: Dolores Bononi, Christine Hardy, Cathy Galarneau, Meghan Devine, Christina Galarneau, Nestor Pangan and Ashlee Harrison. From the Archdiocese of Los Angeles, thanks to Msgr. Francis Weber, Archivist, Kevin Feeney, Adjunct Archivist for access to the Archdiocesan Archives; *The Tidings*, and Catholic Charities of Los Angeles. Additional help came from the Daughters of Charity Historical Conservancy, Holy Family Adoption Service, Franciscan Friars, and Old Mission Santa Barbara Archives.

I am so appreciative of the artistic efforts of illustrator Linda Rowley Blue for the contribution of her original artwork for this publication and for photos from Roe Ann White Photography and John Dlugolecki Photography.

Putting a book together from a variety of sources is no easy task, but I am deeply indebted to those who braved the reading of the manuscript and offering such useful suggestions to help best convey a story of love. My thanks go to Lacy David, Michael Bowman-Jones, and those involved with St. Anne's: Tony Walker, MA, Andy Bogen, Tom Owenson, Steve Gunther and Father William Brand, OFM.

The heart of St. Anne's story is told best by several contributors who wrote their own moving experiences and special accounts of their history with St. Anne's: Afrodita Fuentes, Joan Leslie Caldwell, Machelle Massey, Frances Morehart, Tom Owenson, Yecica Robles, Sandra Romero, Joyce Walter, Tony Walker, Dr. Clyde Von der Ahe, and posthumously, Sister Mary Winifred Falker and Loretta Young Lewis. I also appreciated the words of Sister Mary Elizabeth Imler, OSF, Andrew Bogen, and Father William Brand.

Finally, I want to thank the Centennial Committee whose year-long planning and direction helped to celebrate in great style St. Anne's Century of Service—A Legacy of Love.

Sister Christine, osf

Introduction

Dear Friends of St. Anne's,

May the peace of our gracious God be yours!

Over the course of a century, an institution sees many changes. A good institution rides the wave while a great institution adapts and directs her course. Such is the legacy of St. Anne's. It has gone from simple beginnings to broader adaptations for the times, while remaining true to her mission of responding to women in need. Though the bricks and mortar of the institution may have changed, at the heart of this mission are the people who have cared, given and received ever so constantly. The stories captured in this book record the generous outpouring of time and energy given unconditionally. As we embark on the next century, we, the Franciscan Sisters of the Sacred Heart, stand in thanksgiving for all who, like St. Anne, the grandmother of Jesus, model for the next generation to give their all simply out of love.

A "hundred"-fold of blessings to each of you!

Congratulations and heartfelt thanks,

Peace,
Sister Mary Elizabeth

Sister Mary Elizabeth, O.S.F.
General Superior,
and all the Franciscan Sisters of the Sacred Heart

Andrew E. Bogen

About 1989, I was asked by an extraordinary woman, Sister Margaret Anne Floto of the Franciscan Sisters of the Sacred Heart, if I would consider joining the Board of Directors of St. Anne's Maternity Home. Until that time, I had not known about St. Anne's. Sr. Margaret Anne explained that after decades as a traditional maternity home and maternity hospital, St. Anne's had recently completed a strategic planning process and was undergoing a substantial change.

St. Anne's had embarked on a major construction project: replacement of its residential facility, and creating a new program to serve pregnant and parenting girls in Los Angeles County protective services—foster care and probation. Subsequent phases of the long term plan included the closure of Glassell Street, which then bisected St. Anne's campus, construction of new facilities and the development of new services including a childcare center. St. Anne's had also decided to expand the board with new members, representative of a cross-section of the community. It sounded like an exciting and challenging long term plan.

In 1999, I had the privilege of becoming the Chairman of St. Anne's board, the first layman to hold that position.

It has been my pleasure to be a part of the community as St. Anne's has evolved and dramatically expanded into its role as a leader in Southern California to serve impoverished young pregnant and parenting women, their children and families. The young women who served at St. Anne's share:

- ❈ childhood histories of extreme instability, neglect and abuse
- ❈ the profound experience of having become pregnant as young teenagers without supportive husbands or families
- ❈ the potential of becoming successful adults, but also a high risk of tragic failure for themselves and their children

In addition to its residential treatment program, St. Anne's is now providing housing opportunities for girls leaving the foster care and probation systems, quality childcare for single working mothers, parenting and literacy instruction, mental health and family-based services. St. Anne's is contributing to successful outcomes—directly for the individuals it serves, and indirectly to many more by the development of new models for effective services. St. Anne's also contributes significantly to the revitalization and rekindling of hope in one of Los Angeles' neediest communities.

All this is possible thanks to ten decades of leadership and support from a broad community of staff, volunteers, and public organizations and agencies—both religious and not. In this, St. Anne's centennial year, it is fitting to remember and honor those who played special roles in the development of St. Anne's.

That is the purpose of this book.

Andrew E. Bogen

Andrew E. Bogen, Chairman, St. Anne's Board of Directors

Prologue

Sister Mary Winifred Falker, a Franciscan Sister of the Sacred Heart, was first "missioned" to a little maternity hospital, traveling from the Midwest to Los Angeles. She wrote down some of her early reflections:

> Sister Madeleine Williams and I first arrived at this tiny hospital in January of 1941; I had only $37 in my pocket but my heart was full with the desire to see the mission and philosophies of the Franciscan Sisters fulfilled. But I had no idea what I was getting into!
>
> The rooms in this ten-bed facility were very meagerly furnished at the time and the hospital equipment was obsolete and inefficient. I felt our work was cut out for us: implementing the means by which we could ensure management of a first class hospital. The initial visit was less than encouraging or even inviting. The Superintendent, Marie Campbell, greeted us graciously enough but there appeared to be fear and perhaps resentment on the faces of the nurses.
>
> And oh, the three-day journey to get here! On January 1, 1941, there was a huge downpour when we waved a farewell to our Sisters who braved the storm to say 'goodbye' when Sister Madeleine and Reverend Mother Johanna Reiplinger and I boarded the Golden State Limited in Joliet, Illinois, bound for the City of Angels.

Familiar with the work of the Sisters at Queen of Angels Hospital, Archbishop Cantwell begged, prayed and gently persuaded Mother

Johanna to accept this opportunity to extend the Franciscans' work of mercy to the unfortunate.

On the evening of January 3, 1941, the three weary nuns were met at the station by two of the Franciscan Sisters, Sisters Alberta and Susanna, who took them to their beautiful hospital, Queen of Angels, which stood on the hill overlooking the City of Los Angeles. Sister Winifred prayed:

What a beautiful sight it was viewing the city from the hilltop. O Mary, Queen of Angels, watch over us! Intercede on behalf of us with your Son to bless the work we are about to undertake.

Sister Winifred recollected what happened next:

The very next morning, Mother Johanna, the General Superior of the Franciscan Sisters, took Sister Madeleine and me to the little institution called St Anne's, located at 2814 Council Street, to undertake one of the greatest works of mercy and charitable undertakings, namely the care of unwed mothers.

An early typewritten chronicle stated: "This small group of brave souls was destined by Divine Providence to add another chapter to the Order's interesting archives of accomplishments."

And so it was….

What began as a small 12-bed hospital was to grow into an institution, the only one of its class in the United States. It really was "one of a kind."

Part One

THE EARLY YEARS
1908-1938

In 1908, Bishop Thomas J. Conaty of the Monterey-Los Angeles Diocese, rented a beautiful mansion at 1503 South Figueroa for the purpose of establishing a maternity hospital for married and unmarried women. He had long desired such a facility, especially one devoted to the poor.

Bishop Conaty was particularly touched by the dilemma of unwed mothers as it was in 1908. They were shunned as outcasts and often had nowhere to turn for help. Stories of babies born in such places as the Old Plaza Park or behind the Old Mission, urged Bishop Conaty to take action. Unwed mothers managed alone, heartbroken and often ill. Society's disregard for them was made more intolerable by the shame and disgrace heaped upon them. They received very little sympathy, compassion, kindness or love.[1]

THE ST. ROSE GUILD

The Guild (founded in April 1907) was a significant society that assisted the first St. Anne's Maternity Hospital. Since the guild was composed of Catholic nurses, Bishop Conaty was able to select experienced nurses from this group who would devote themselves to the hospital. Miss Agnes Donnelly was the first President of the St. Rose Guild and Miss Mary Frances McDonald, its founding secretary. The

3

Honorable Joseph Scott was very active in aiding this guild and he was instrumental in establishing St. Anne's Guild thirty years later. The St. Rose Guild was organized primarily to aid the St. Vincent de Paul Conferences; its special purpose was to furnish nurses for emergency charitable cases.

Dr. William R. Malony, who served at the request of Bishop Conaty, was an adviser to St. Rose's Guild and one of the original volunteers on the staff of St. Anne's. His service spanned the first 65 years of the hospital and continued after retirement with the Joachim League, a men's volunteer organization at St. Anne's.[2]

THE FIRST ST. ANNE'S

The maternity hospital was dedicated on November 6th, 1908. *The Tidings*, the diocesan newspaper, reported: "St. Anne's Maternity Hospital has been very thoroughly fitted with the most complete and up to date equipment for its work. No expense has been spared in preparing for the comfort and convenience

The first St. Anne's – 1908
Fifteenth & Figueroa

of the patients. The hospital has comfortable accommodations for twelve patients and is in the charge of two skilled graduate nurses, Miss Mary Frances McDonald and Miss Agnes Donnelly." (See Notes, page 113)

Bishop Conaty proudly captured what St. Anne's is all about:

The establishment of St. Anne's Maternity Hospital was an answer to a demand for this special class of work among the sick, and although the work was begun in a simple way to meet immediate

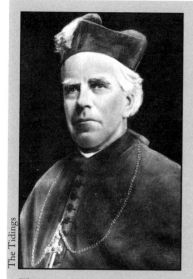

The Tidings

BISHOP THOMAS J. CONATY
1903–1915

Bishop Conaty had just completed a six-year term as rector of Catholic University of America when he was appointed head of the See of Monterey-Los Angeles and served in that capacity from 1903-1915. One of his major interests was Catholic education and preserving mission churches. He organized the St. Vincent de Paul Society and in 1904, acquired The Tidings as the official diocesan publication. During his episcopate, the total population of the diocese doubled. In addition to 229 priests, many new orders of Sisters were serving the diocese in education, hospitals and orphanages. When he died in 1915, the Catholic population in the Diocese had grown to 178,000, three times the number when he came to the Diocese.

demands, I am satisfied that in time it would develop into a large institution of which the community would be proud.

St. Anne's Maternity Hospital is blessed today in the name of Christ and under the patronage of St. Anne, the mother of the Blessed Virgin. It enters into the institutional life of this community in the broad spirit of helpfulness toward those who are in need of its care. It adds another link in the chain of charitable institutions which the Catholic Church maintains in Los Angeles, and under our direction it will, like all our other institutions of charity, be governed entirely by the good it may be able to do.

We pray God to bless it in its work, to bless the physicians who attend the sick and the nurses who kindly care for them, so that Los Angeles may have another source of blessing in whatever good it will be capable of doing for suffering womankind.

Bishop Conaty's comments were almost prophetic as the great work of this institution was to be known in the decades to come. Indeed, it did become another link in the chain of charitable institutions doing such good work. Bishop Conaty established an admission criterion: "The only entrance condition it exacts is the need of its service. No religious or race lines will ever be allowed to prevent it from doing good to any woman who may demand it."[3]

The admission standard remains the same today.

Thus began St. Anne's. The day after its dedication, one of the first babies listed in the hospital was a baby girl, daughter of Mr. and Mrs. Daniel Hurley from Boston. The baby was named Anne.[4]

A celebration in 1909 marked the first anniversary of St. Anne's Maternity Hospital. Thirty-four distinguished doctors attended the festivities. Within the first year, a host of Catholic physicians agreed to donate their time and expertise to the hospital. Bishop Conaty was delighted that the physicians of the city had responded to his appeals. Each doctor pledged a month's service in rotation. The Bishop developed the practice that the hospital would be open to all reputable physicians and the management of the hospital was directed by the nurses who were selected for that purpose. They held their authority directly from the Bishop, who thus became responsible for the maintenance of the hospital.

During the first year of operation, little St. Anne's

St. Anne's – 1508 S. Figueroa
Interior view – 1908

served 82 patients with 67 births, including two sets of twins. They came from a variety of religious backgrounds: 34% Catholic, 30% Protestant denominations, 4.8% were Jewish, and the remainder "other." The Bishop's admission criterion was working.

Over the next ten years, St. Anne's services to unwed mothers continued at various locations, each time changing its name to fit the emphasis on services. The first move was to Glendale, then to Los Angeles, Highland Park, Hollywood and then finally back to Los Angeles in 1921. The detail of these moves and name changes can be found in the Notes section, pages 113-114.

St. Anne's grew, but in 1915 the staff at the home experienced real personal loss with the death of its founder and advocate, Bishop Conaty, who did not live long enough to bless the new facility in Hollywood.

The move to Hollywood was important for eventually it created involvement of the of the motion picture industry. One of the first actresses to be associated with the institution was Polly Moran who

St. Anne's Infant Home – Glendale, 1912

A HINT OF HOLLYWOOD

By Joan Leslie Caldwell

I can remember quite vividly when I first became associated with St. Anne's. It was Christmas Eve, 1949. Dr. Caldwell, my soon to be husband, was a volunteer on the staff for many years. He had arranged with Sister Winifred for us to attend Midnight Mass. The churches weren't doing that too much in Los Angeles, and so it was a special time. He brought his mother and father and me. I think we were sort of engaged. Anyway, he brought me to St. Anne's. The tiny chapel was exquisitely decorated for the holiday. There was that lovely feeling of Christmas in the halls. The most inspirational moment to me was at Communion where every single one of the girls went to Communion, too. They were all dressed in crisp white blouses and pinafores, but with tummies way out to here, expecting, every one of them. To see them go up the aisle and receive Communion was an incredibly moving sight. So I became extremely interested and quite curious; I simply had to know more about St. Anne's.

In 1954, Sister Winifred asked me to go onto the Board of Trustees. I said to her, "I can't possibly do that; I have two little girls, and I am still working in pictures!" I didn't think I could possibly handle it. Then I heard who was on the board—impressive: lawyers, business men, judges, doctors, and social leaders. I thought, "How could I possibly help?" All those marvelous people are on the board! Where could I possibly fit in? But eventually when I agreed, I learned a great deal from these wonderful people, who were so devoted. It was a joy to work with them and to think with them about what could be done for the girls at St. Anne's. I can't imagine that I am now St. Anne's oldest living board member!

Two aspects that are extremely satisfying about the institution: one is seeing the babies being lovingly and safely delivered, and the other is knowing that their mothers will have an opportunity for a better life, with possibilities they couldn't even imagine without St. Anne's. It is gratifying when you talk to one or two of the girls and they tell you how they feel about their lives and their babies' lives. These young mothers are just children themselves, of course, when they arrive. They have no idea about how to handle a baby—how to put on a diaper, or how to be patient. So they need a lot of direction, as well as nurturing and education so they can grow. I think they do grow and learn; the nurturing and education is really important for their babies. So, to see these young women mature under the care of the wonderfully trained people who can help them is incredibly rewarding. They need a helping hand, and they're getting it here.

Over the years many celebrities have contributed their time and talent to St. Anne's. Loretta Young, for example, was very involved. At one point, Sister Winifred asked her to be chairman of our board and to my amazement, given Loretta's hectic schedule, the actress accepted wholeheartedly. She not only presided at board meetings, but if there were fundraising events like an afternoon tea or an elegant dinner party, she would bring celebrities from the entertainment world. It would make for an especially remarkable evening to have her walk in with Irene Dunne, Rosalind Russell, and Charlton Heston—all well known movie stars at the time. She brought them to a dinner party we had at the Beverly Hills Hotel. I remember she was dancing with Charlton Heston, and I was dancing with my husband and when I met Mr. Heston, I thought, I'm just not tall enough to see his face!! He was an extremely handsome and gracious man; just one of Loretta's good friends, like Ruth Roman and Caesar Romero. It was quite exciting for everyone at the dinner party to see these movie stars we only saw in pictures.

Celebrities are very generous, usually. If you approach them the right way, they will take a genuine interest in your charity. Ann Blyth has been very active with us, as well as Tippi Hedrin, Jane Withers, Margaret O'Brien, Pat Boone, Art Linkletter, and Roddy McDowell. These wonderful Hollywood stars brought a touch of glamour to many of our St. Anne's events. But the real "star" was Sister Winifred. She was unique. Sister Winifred had good religious sense, of course, but she had good business sense and good common sense, too. She had keen judgment and remarkable foresight to see the future needs of St. Anne's—and she was right! But with all that, she was a warm, charming person who drew people to her who could help.

All the doctors on the staff were devoted to her; they loved her directness and dedication. Although obstetricians like my husband, William, and colleagues Clyde Von der Ahe, Bob Kelly, and Jim Kelly, were busy supporting their families, when Sister Winifred called them, they came. They may have put in a full day of seeing their private patients and then be up all night at St. Anne's delivering a baby! But they would never ignore Sister Winifred's heartfelt requests.

When Sister first asked me to go on the board, I was awfully reluctant; I said "no" several times. After a while I thought I would just stay at St. Anne's until the problem of unwed pregnancy was solved! I certainly was naïve! But the problem grew, and we had to respond to that, and we did. I'm quite proud of being a part of St. Anne's. I think we grew with the problem because we had to. There are different aspects to it, and it's more demanding than it ever was. But we are here for those girls.

adopted a baby boy from St. Anne's. Marie Dressler was also generous to the home. This set the stage for others in Hollywood to become actively involved throughout the decades.

In June 1916, Miss M. E. Campbell was the third nurse to join Misses Donnelly and McDonald in their charitable work at St. Anne's. A sewing circle had been formed to assist the nurses caring for the children. For the first time, the Feast of St. Anne, patron of the home, was celebrated. Eventually this became a time-honored tradition in St. Anne's history.

Agnes Donnelly, one of the original nurses at St. Anne's, on her 90th birthday, February 4, 1962

St. Anne's Infant Home was finally blessed on January 18, 1918 by the Most Reverend John J. Cantwell. He followed his predecessor by expressing great interest in the work at St. Anne's. But in April, the Hollywood facility was directed to close when it was determined that the home would come under the direction of the Catholic Welfare Bureau (later known as Catholic Charities). This Bureau was formally organized in 1919.

Bishop Cantwell moved the St. Anne's operation in 1921 to a small frame building at 1044 North Mariposa Street and renamed the facility St. Vincent's Hospital and Home.[5] Little information is available about the facility during the next two decades, though the facility on Mariposa Street was to endure until 1938. Initially, it provided hospital care for both married and unmarried mothers who were unable to pay regular hospital fees. But by 1924, the home was used exclusively for the care of unwed mothers.

A brochure about it stated: "For many years St. Vincent's Maternity Home has carried on a high type of care of unmarried mothers and their babies, and merited the commendation of the Social Service

Commission, the Council of Social Agencies, and the State Department of Public Health. Referrals came from Catholic Welfare Bureau, Juvenile Courts, Bureaus of County Welfare, and nonsectarian agencies throughout Southern California. Some 2,300 mothers and babies were cared for during the years. And by 1930, the home was accommodating twenty-six mothers and ten babies."[6]

In 1937, the Catholic Welfare Bureau acquired property at 155 North Occidental Boulevard that covered a city block bounded by Occidental, Reno, and Council Streets plus Glassell Place. At first, St. Anne's took up occupancy on Occidental in two one-story fireproof buildings: the hospital had a capacity for 10 mothers and 20 babies and the other contained a dining room, finely equipped kitchen and quarters for the nursing and medical staffs.

The facility moved to its permanent location in 1938, the year that St. Anne's Guild was formed, at 155 North Occidental Boulevard and again named *St. Anne's Maternity Hospital.*

So WHO was St. Anne?

St. Anne Mother of Mary, Grandmother of Jesus

In a delightful book by Francis Parkinson Keys, *St. Anne—Grandmother of Our Saviour,* the author tells us that "Our Lord had a grandmother, too. Anne was human in every aspect of the word and is a true model for all women. Mary, her daughter, was set apart because of Mary's exaltation with the Immaculate Conception, virgin motherhood, and glorious Assumption. It is thought that Anne's husband and father were men who were very well off."[7]

Anne and her husband, Joachim, deserve honor. In the United States, 400 churches are dedicated to St. Anne, as well as the many shrines and churches in other parts of the world.

Excerpts from the Spring 2001 issue of the *Angel Messenger* tell a little more about St. Anne:

THE ELUSIVE ST. ANNE

By Father William Brand, OFM

Have you ever wondered about St. Anne, whose name we bear? If you have, you're not by yourself.

Well, if you are looking it up in your Bible, don't waste your time. If you are looking her up in a Book of Saints, you might find some spotty information. At best, she is elusive.

The Apocryphal book, the *Protoevangelium Jacopi* (or *Gospel of James*) written about the year A.D. 170 tells us all we know about the grandparents of Jesus. That's right, the grandparents of Jesus! According to the story, Joachim was a prominent and respected man, who had no children. He and his wife, Anne, looked upon this as a punishment from God, which was the normal mindset of their day. In answer to their prayers, Mary was born and dedicated to God at a very early age, later to become the Mother of God, Jesus.

While the Church never accepted the Gospel of James as canonical, meaning not worthy of the Biblical collection that we now use and enjoy, the account was definitely a part of the stories of Jesus that circulated in early Christian communities.

Joachim and Anne—whether these are their real names or not—represent that quiet series of generations, those who faithfully perform their duties, practice their faith, and establish an atmosphere for coming of the Messiah, but remain obscure. A joint feast, celebrated on September 9th, originated in the Orient near the end of the sixth century. Devotion to Anne, introduced in the eighth century in Rome, became widespread in Europe in the 14th century. Her feast was given to the Catholic Church worldwide in 1584. The feast of St. Joachim was celebrated in early times by the Greeks and about the fifteenth century by the Romans.

St. Anne's feast day is July 26th and St. Joachim was celebrated in various months, September, March or December. Today, with the revision of the Roman calendar, she and her husband are celebrated together. From the observance of St. Anne's feast has come the celebration of the Immaculate Conception, the Nativity of Mary, and the Annunciation.

Many believe that the church of St. Anne in Jerusalem was built on the site of Anne and Joachim's home. Of the many chapels and churches dedicated to St. Anne, perhaps the most famous is the Shrine of St. Anne de Beaupre near Quebec in Canada. Many miracles have been attributed to her at that shrine.

So many of our residents need a loving grandparent. It is fitting that St. Anne should be the name chosen for our facility.

ST. ANNE'S HOSPITAL GUILD

This was the first organization to support the work of St. Anne's, and was fortunate to have Mrs. George L. Humphreys as the founding president. Within a year, the Guild held its first annual bazaar.

In 1944, the Guild opened its first thrift shop on Temple Street in Los Angeles, chaired by Mrs. Walter Luer. Originally, the Guild members staffed the shop only on Fridays and picked up all the donations as did Sister Winifred herself! By 1947, a full time worker was hired for Saturdays. Over the years,

*Mrs. George L. Humphreys,
Founder 1938-1945*

circumstances required the shop to move six times in order to accommodate the increased donations and the need for more space. (See Notes, pages 114-115)

The Guild operated another business known as Venture III, which opened in the 1970's and continued until the early 1980's. The Wilshire Boulevard store sold antiques, collectibles and new merchandise.

In 1982, a second economy shop opened in North Hollywood on Magnolia Boulevard that ran concurrently with the Los Angeles store. After the Temple Street shop closed, the final location for Los Angeles was the Weingart Building on Beverly Boulevard and Reno

St. Anne's Economy Shop –
Circa 1950s

Street which finally closed in 1993. By 2008, the North Hollywood shop still continued its successful operation.

The Guild has had a significant influence in the history of St. Anne's. Its contributions of volunteer hours and financial support are stellar. The Bazaars, Day at the Races, dinner auctions, fashion shows, garage sales, luncheons, card parties, and Venture III have raised over $3 million for St. Anne's, and contributed over one million hours of service to the ministry. The Guild and its volunteers were first recognized in May of 1969 with an angel pin at the annual "Tea and Talk" function. The pin was initially designed by Mrs. Jerri Schreck Stell. The "angel award" was the precursor to the Evening of Angels, which evolved into St. Anne's annual award gala.[8]

What a history St. Anne's had for those thirty years, fulfilling its mission to pregnant women remained the same. And 1941 ushered in a fresh new era for the little maternity home.

St. Anne's Guild - 1998

Seated on Floor: Pat Mattison, Joan Broderick, Joan Leslie Caldwell, Eleanor Mancinelli, Dolores Bononi, Joan Potthast, Lois Bisenius, Mary Byrne

Seated: Pat Kearin, Mary Crehan, Dominica Tierney, Mary Schoenfeldt, Maria Raia, Catherine Winnek, Haydee Conkey, Mary Dohn, Anita Torreano

Standing: Marie Folin, Bette Hawkins, Clare James Cronin, Marilyn Meichtry, Helen Cobb, Myrtis Butler, Joan Shewfelt, Vickie Richards, Connie Reese, Jeanine Bartusch, Helen Cecil, Frances Morehart, Peggy Leoni, Kay Reid, Raymonde Bardeau, Yvonne Bononi, Rosemary Marco, Margaret Chambers, Caroline Rodela, Marjorie Ellen Pryor, Irene Montgomery, Emily Rosso, Ann Brunner

Part Two

1941: A NEW ERA
Arrival of the Franciscan Sisters of the Sacred Heart

Sister Winifred continued the description of her early days at St. Anne's:

Archbishop Cantwell called for a meeting. Mother Johannah, Sister Madeleine, Sister Alberta and I met with him and discussed the details of the transfer to the Franciscan Sisters. Oh, the Archbishop was so delighted that we were there; he once again expressed his gratitude,

Front Entrance –
Sisters Winifred and Madeleine

happiness, and appreciation to Reverend Mother Johanna for her kindness in sending us to his little hospital.

Since we had no means of transportation to get back and forth from St. Anne's to Queen of Angels Hospital, we appealed to the kindness of the Archbishop to see if he had an old jalopy or something we could use. To our surprise, the Archbishop sent a brand new Plymouth Sedan! That was a Godsend!

The next few weeks went very well and mutual understanding and cooperation marked

First car given by Archbishop Cantwell

the day. It was a newly constructed ten-bed maternity hospital which opened in 1938 on the Occidental Blvd site. The buildings and property were transferred to the Franciscan Sisters. The Sisters officially began their work on March 1, 1941. And we were undaunted by the challenge before us; we set out to do what was ours to do. With just two Sisters in charge, the going was pretty rough.

Since we had no formal convent at the time, there was not even a room to call our own. I remember that we didn't even have beds but Sister Alberta from Queen of Angels donated a couple of large arm chairs. Each night we moved reclining chairs from one spot to another, wherever we could find space, in order to get our rest. Boards across the chairs became our makeshift beds! We had a single room that served as dormitory, recreation and chapel all at once.[9]

With amazing aplomb, Sister Winifred moved quickly to accomplish as much as possible for the new ministry of the Franciscan Sisters.

DEVELOPMENT OF ST. ANNE'S

Sister Winifred had the facility formally incorporated on March 13, 1941. In the same month, the first medical staff was organized with eminent physicians Alphonsus M. McCarthy, Walter Holleran, T.J.

The Tidings

ARCHBISHOP JOHN J. CANTWELL
BISHOP 1917–1936,
ARCHBISHOP 1936–1947

Two major divisions of the Monterey-Los Angeles Diocese occurred during the time of Archbishop Cantwell. His was the longest term—30 years. In 1922, Pope Pius XI approved the division of the 90,000 square-mile diocese and created the Diocese of Los Angeles-San Diego. The next major alteration occurred in 1936 with the erection of a second Metropolitan District in California at Los Angeles with the four southernmost counties comprising the Diocese of San Diego. Bishop Cantwell became the first archbishop, to be noted for his provision for the spiritual and material welfare of the non-English speaking people. He created 50 Hispanic parishes and missions and died in 1947.

O'Neill, and Clement Malony who were among its charter members. Dr. McCarthy served as chief of staff and all medical care was under his direct supervision. Resident physicians from the Queen of Angels Hospital assisted Dr. McCarthy to provide the necessary medical care for the girls in residence. Sister Winifred wrote:

> The need for a place to shelter the Sisters was great. Sister Alberta even donated two bungalows so that we could arrange suitable living quarters. As "charming" as the multipurpose room was that we had been

Old Cottage, Glassel Street – 1941

using for weeks, a more permanent home would be wonderful. We spent many hours pouring over possibilities of remodeling the cottages to accommodate our needs. On the advice of my brother, Elmer Joseph Falker, we sold the bungalows and used the proceeds toward a new building which netted $900. With this money, a loan of $3,000 from the Archbishop, $2,000 from the Motherhouse, along with the whole-hearted approval of superiors and planning authorities, we drew up plans for a new building.[10]

Sister Winifred was never one to hesitate and her initial days at St. Anne's were filled with activity. Only thirteen days after St. Anne's was formally incorporated on March 13, 1941, the first of many ground-breakings during her tenure took place. On March 26th, construction began of a small 40 by 60 square foot building called "The Annex." It included a chapel, bedrooms for the Sisters and rooms for four girls. Initially heavy rains slowed the progress but the Sisters were undeterred. (See Notes, page 115)

The first outpatient department was opened on April 3, 1941 to give prenatal care to the residents of the hospital and clinic attendance rose rapidly.

A couple of months later on June 29th, the chronicles described a memorable day at the hospital: the new chapel had been sufficiently finished to permit the celebration of the Holy Sacrifice of the Mass. This was an important event in the lives of the Sisters and staff. The privilege of the first Mass was accorded to the pious Reverend John J. Wehmhoefer who had been a patient at Queen of Angels Hospital and was recruited for the Mass.

Chapel – 1941

FRANCISCAN SISTERS OF THE SACRED HEART

For over 130 years the Franciscan Sisters of the Sacred Heart have provided works of neighborly love wherever God has called us to be.

Our history is long. In the providence of God and inspired by Father Wilhelm Berger, three daring women in Seelbach, Germany, accepted the challenge to serve the poor, the sick, and the aging of their village in 1866. From this small group grew the congregation now known as the Franciscan Sisters of the Sacred Heart. In those early days, the Sisters spent long hours serving people in physical and spiritual need. When the climate in Germany changed during the "Kurturkampf," the Sisters were forced to disband or leave the country. With deep faith they sought guidance in prayer. Before making a final decision, the Rev. Dominic Duehmig invited Mother Anastasia Bischler and the Sisters to America. In 1876, they arrived in Indiana and settled in Avilla. Later the Sisters established their Motherhouse in Illinois, first in Joliet and now at its present location in Frankfort. The vision of the early Sisters continues to inspire the present members to dedicated lives of service.

Our love is deep. The Sisters continue to serve wherever they are called, responding to the needs of God's people. Their founder, Father Wilhelm Berger, envisioned Sisters who, with a commitment to the ideals of St. Vincent de Paul, would do "works of neighborly love" in the spirit of Francis and Clare of Assisi.

The Sisters serve in hospitals, clinics, social service agencies, and support programs for pregnant and parenting teens. They bring Christ to others through spiritual direction, bodywork, and retreats. They minister as teachers, administrators, and religious education coordinators. They serve as pastoral associates and in diocesan offices. They sponsor the Portiuncula Center for Prayer in Frankfort, and St. Anne's Maternity Home in Los Angeles. They co-sponsor seven hospitals, fifteen long-term care facilities, and over forty clinics in Indiana and Illinois through Provena Health. They also serve in Brazil, South America.

The Sisters created the Poverello Holistic Center within a charming and rustic house on the grounds of St. Francis Woods. There, the needs of body, mind and spirit are attended to through various modalities of bodywork. This bodywork is available to the general public and to guests at the Portiuncula Center for Prayer. Woodsong Music Ministries is also hosted at St. Francis Woods that uses the power of music to change hearts, to heal the body, mind and soul, to spiritually energize people, and to bring them into the harmony of God.

Our faith is firm. Following in the footsteps of our founders and pioneer Sisters, we endeavor to remain faithful to our heritage. We are especially inspired by their prayerful discernment of God's will and their daring response to it, their willingness to go wherever they were needed, their incredible trust in Divine Providence, their determination to live in community despite danger, and their seeking guidance from the Church. These are our roots that, following the Spirit's lead, we firmly seek to live out in the changing conditions of our times.

Our hopes are high. Our Franciscan heritage reminds us that the Spirit called us together to continue the mission of Jesus. Regularly we gather at our home, the Motherhouse, which nourishes and gives growth to the heart ad spirit of our congregation. It is from this center that we are sent forth to minister. It is to this center that we come to celebrate Professions, Jubilees, and community gatherings; to seek solitude; and to renew friendships. It is also to this center that we return when our bodies can no longer bear the demands of ministry and our spirits lead us into the ministry of prayer. Knowing that we have this home sustains us in "always being eager to observe what we have promised the Lord." (Blessing of St. Clare).

Our vision is wide. When the Sisters first arrived in American in 1876, it was evident that the new neighbors needed the Sisters as much as the Sisters needed them! Today's world still longs for this neighborly love.

Our mission is to respond to our neighbors in need.
Our **vision** is to be the gentle hands and the beating hearts of Jesus.
Our **joy** is to be with our neighbors.
www.fssh.com

(Excerpts from the *125th Anniversary Booklet of the Franciscan Sisters of the Sacred Heart*)

July 4, 1941 saw another type of independence day at St. Anne's: the Sisters finally moved into their new home. Gone were the makeshift beds in the crowded multipurpose room. In addition to the new space, the Sisters were blessed with several surprises of useful gifts from many benefactors. Time and time again in the years to come, the Sisters would have reason to give thanks to God for the generosity of their benefactors who not only made the work they were called to do more pleasant, but the mission of St. Anne's possible.

During the month of September, the practice of using beds solely for the care of indigent unmarried women was inaugurated. Sister Winifred also received permission to sell approximately ten lots facing Glassell, Reno, and Council Streets for $10,000. This seemed like "Manna from Heaven." It enabled the Sisters to pay their normal operating expenses for the first time, to liquidate their debts and to purchase more food of different varieties for the patients.

The Franciscan Sisters made great progress at St. Anne's. Just in time for Christmas, the newly completed chapel was dedicated on December 21st by the Right Reverend Monsignor John Cawley, FAVG, assisted by Reverend Raymond J. O'Flaherty, Right Reverend Msgr. T. J. O'Dwyer, and Reverend Charles Knebel, O.F.M. This was a fitting close to St. Anne's first year.

In 1942, the Sisters and Medical Staff received written confirmation that St. Anne's received its first Accreditation by the American College of Surgeons, a sign of excellence for the hospital. For all the years of its existence, the hospital maintained its accreditation and was the only accredited hospital west of St. Louis that was physically located in a maternity home.

They achieved another milestone on June 16, 1945 with the groundbreaking for a new wing. Sister Winifred chronicled the event:

The 1946 wing expanded the services of St. Anne's. This 12,000 square foot expansion opened in January. This wonderful new addition brought the bed capacity up to thirty-five with twenty bassinets. Included in the new wing were a new chapel and sacristy, chaplain's quarters, audi-

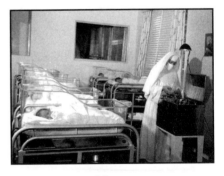

Nursery

torium, recreation room, parlor, dental laboratory, two clinical examination rooms, dressing room, five single and nine double bedrooms. The old chapel was converted into administrative offices. At the same time, extensive improvements to the gardens were made. A Lourdes Grotto and outdoor Stations of the Cross were erected.

These additions added to the spiritual life of the Sisters and staff and were a means of prayer and devotion.

*Sacred Heart Patio –
Sisters Borromeo, Siena,
Thomasine, Madeline and
Winifred*

*Standing: Sr. Carmelita Dominguez, Sr. Mary
Joan Miller, Sr. Joanita Grochowski, Sr. Elaine
Grochowski; Seated: Sr. Winifred Falker,
Sr. Rosalia Fueglister, Sr. Borromeo Feier*

Sister Carmelita Dominguez

Sister Mary Joan Miller

Sister Borromeo Feier

The first full time social worker was hired in January 1946. That year, 247 patients were admitted. All non-resident cases, married or unmarried, became the responsibility of the Catholic Welfare Bureau and were to be financed through St. Anne's by the Bureau. A case worker was assigned to St. Anne's and had exclusive control over the cases that came to the institution, independent of the Bureau, as directed by the Most Reverend Timothy Manning, then Auxiliary Bishop of Los Angeles.[11]

St. Anne's Front Entrance – 1946

The formal dedication of the new wing was held on April 7th by His Excellency, the Most Reverend John J. Cantwell, Archbishop of Los Angeles. Sister Winifred wrote:

*St. Anne's Front Entrance – 1946
Annex to the left*

Alexander Kahle

At the time, we felt that we surely were going to have plenty of space for the next ten to fifteen years. I still remember, in January of 1946 moving into our spacious girls' dormitory containing 36 beds. We had a lovely little chapel; and the present administrative offices were, at that time, our clinic rooms. What rejoicing. Thirty-six little mothers with thirty-six little

Sister Mary Winifred on front porch

babes nestling under their hearts to care for and to start on a way of life that would lead to future happiness. Soon the two bedrooms gave way to three bedrooms. Cottages came into existence and bed capacity rose to fifty-two. Other community leaders' strong hearts and arms were: Dr. George Piness, Fritz Burns, Charles Dunn, Harold McAlister, Henry Gogerty, and Judge Guerin.

Chapel, Side View – 1946
Our Lady of Lourdes Patio

However, almost overnight it seemed, the place was filled up with girls from every corner of the city and county. Business was booming! The load was heavy, and,

Girls Prenatal Outpatient Rooms – 1946

with little help, very, very difficult. But it was all worthwhile when we looked into the eyes of a grateful woman and listened to her words of gratitude and her promises to ask Almighty God to bless those who helped her through her agony. It was all worthwhile, too, when the infant, a precious soul of God's creation, was placed in a good home, with loving parents and a wonderful opportunity to be raised as a good and honorable member of society.[12]

THE UNWED MOTHER IN THE 1940'S

Here is a snapshot of the challenges the unwed mother faced in 1946 from the booklet, *The Gracious Story of St. Anne's.*[13]

By the time she has arrived in the shelter of St. Anne's, she has become an extremely harassed human being. The future life she has envisioned is tragic. Not only is she alone—she probably has been freshly abandoned, and no human eyes ever should be forced to look alone upon such a problem without a comforter.

She probably is bereft of family and friends. Occasionally, she has been expelled. Most often, however, this separation is voluntary. She seeks to shield her family, her baby and herself from embarrassment. She disengages herself from natural surroundings, thereby cutting herself off from natural channels of assistance.

There are some admirable qualities about the woman who seeks St. Anne's in the hour of her approaching motherhood. Fortitude is one of her characteristics. She may be the victim of a lie, a legal technicality, or an overly generous heart. She may be a dazed girl who has been abused with violence and terror by the maniac. Yet, when face to face with this unexpected and startling situation, she has the bravery and the determination to see it through.

It should be recognized and stated openly, once and for all, that she knows there are alternatives. Some of these alternatives are bitter and ghastly avenues of destruction but they also offer secrecy for her. Those less brave, those less inspired, and those less commendable, those with less understanding and foresight and guidance—seek the misery and malfeasance of the abortionist.

The girl who reaches the door of St. Anne's may be pitifully young, extremely poor. She bears the marks of fresh shock. She realizes she is responsible for two lives with an uncertain future in a busy and preoccupied society, a society which, by and large, does not know or care about her predicament and, if it were made aware, probably would react with hostility, or be indignant, or be embarrassed by her."

Cover of the booklet,
The Gracious Story of
St. Anne's

This little booklet captures the picture of the unwed mother and what she had to face.

It was not a pretty picture but when the young girl enters St. Anne's, all that changes. This is what St. Anne's is all about, the volunteers, the workers, the professionals who give of themselves. These people are the hallmarks of this great institution. Some of these unwed mothers had suffered far too much punishment before reaching St. Anne's. All of the people working on behalf of the young women who come to St. Anne's are building brighter futures for those entrusted to their care.

MAMA'S HOT TAMALES

By Sandra Romero

When I became pregnant at age 14, my mother and grandmother told me I had to give the baby up for adoption. They said I was too young to care for a child and needed to get an education first…. I was the oldest of seven children. My alcoholic stepfather beat my mom and abused me since I was six. My parents heard that St. Anne's was a safe place for me to go have the baby while going to school.

When I first got there, I felt frightened and alone, but after hearing the other girls' stories and getting to know the nuns who were so kind and supportive, I became confident and hopeful that my life could improve. Being there gave me time to think and helped me realize how important education was. Upon giving birth, I took one look at my little girl and decided I could not give her up for adoption. My mother made it perfectly clear that raising this baby was solely my responsibility. At 14, I returned home, took care of my daughter, Christina, and worked hard to finish high school while helping my mom raise my other siblings. I became a stronger person and somehow found the courage to stop the violence to my mom and me.

At age 17, I moved out with three-year old Christina, rented a house with the help of my Uncle, and attended California State University at Northridge. It was a challenging time in my life. I often brought my daughter to class due to limited day care. Christina was a great motivator, and made me want to succeed in giving us a better life.

While in college, I got a job as a receptionist at the Fair Housing Council of San Gabriel Valley. There, I began an 18-year career as Program Director and later, Executive Director. During that time, I became a confident and loving mother and raised Christina with my husband, Ruben; I first met him in 1978 with my best friend Francine, who was married to Ruben's best friend. After 18 years of marriage, Ruben passed away in 1990.

I had reached a crossroads in my life, and my friend, Dr. Joseph Colletti, wanted to start a non-profit organization to help people in the community. We spoke with Bishop Bruno of the Episcopalian Church, who at that time was helping street vendors deal with the challenges of their businesses. Shortly thereafter, Dr. Colletti and I founded the Institute for Urban Research and Development (IURD), which provides programs to help individuals improve their lives. During that time, I opened "Mama's Hot Tamales," which not only served some of LA's most delicious homemade tamales, but also facilitated training and licensing programs for local street vendors through grants awarded to IURD. By 2007, over 1,000 individuals have been trained to become small business entrepreneurs in the restaurant industry thanks to Mama's Hot Tamales, IURD and PACE business schools.

It's been a very rewarding experience, but the best part of my life has been raising my daughter, Christina, and the birth of my grandson, four-year-old Mathieu. In 1995, I met Jorge Luis Plasencia and we were married on March 21, 1997.

As I reflect back on my life, I realize how lucky I was to have had St. Anne's be part of my journey. It was really a salvation for me. St. Anne's provided me with a safe haven to sort out my feelings of becoming a mother so young and gave me the strength and courage to go into the future with my head up high to make a better life for myself and more important for my daughter, Christina. I will always be grateful that St. Anne's wrapped its arms around me and so many others to guide us with respect and dignity in our journey to motherhood and to

help us realize our importance as human beings. I thank St. Anne's for the greatest gift of all—my daughter, Christina!

Mama's Hot Tamales founder and former resident Sandra Romero (far left) and daughter Christina

St. Anne's Foundation

In June, a prominent group of lay men and women met with Sister Winifred to discuss the establishment of a group in support of St. Anne's and her mission. Among them, was the Honorable Joseph Scott. Resulting from the discussion was the St. Anne's Foundation which was incorporated July 30, 1946. It became the capital funding adjunct of the hospital.[14] (See Notes, pages 115-117)

Mr. Thomas Dockweiler functioned as advisor in the establishment of the Foundation and it was the Board of Trustees who then served as the lay advisory board to St. Anne's.

By 1947, St. Anne's had a staff of fourteen physicians who still provided the services of their specialties without charge. Capacity of the home was 36 with 247 admissions for the year. An additional 45 lived outside of the hospital until delivery but then came into the clinic for medical services.[15]

Community Chest

St. Anne's had become a charter member of the Community Chest in 1925. In 1948, chronicles noted that funds for St. Anne's came through the Chest, voluntary contributions and patient receipts. Referrals came from many sources, such as friends, parents, pastors, doctors, private and public agencies, and public announcements. The age range of the girls was 11 to 42 years with the largest group 14 to 22. Any unmarried mother, regardless of age, nationality, creed, color, or disability could be admitted to St. Anne's. Depending on space constraints, a girl could be admitted at any time during her pregnancy to receive the necessary protection, shelter and medical care. The average length of stay was usually three months although some stayed for two weeks and for five or six months. The twenty physicians on staff included eight obstetricians, three pediatricians and members of several medical specialties such as surgery, orthopedics, and psychiatry.

Additional Facility Services

The institution conducted an educational rehabilitation program for the benefit of the teenagers so they could continue their studies. Other classes were conducted in typing, art, millinery, nutrition, home nursing, ceramics, leisure crafts, sewing, and other occupational arts.

Three hundred women in the St. Anne's Hospital Guild assisted the Sisters in the educational program. The public-spirited, philanthropic men and women of St. Anne's Foundation did much to further the hospital's growth and development.

St. Anne's/Holy Family Adoption Service

When the Sisters' arrived in 1941, they soon saw the need for a Catholic adoption agency. In July, St. Anne's Foundation purchased a cottage located on Council Street to house the new St. Anne's Adoption Service. The first organizing meeting of the agency was held on May 31, 1949, and the Articles of Incorporation were duly approved and filed with the Secretary of State in Sacramento.[16] On May 23, 1949, Mrs. Bob Hope was appointed the first President of the Board and Sister M. Thomasine McKinnon became the agency's first Executive Director. In June of 1950, the name of the agency was changed to *Holy Family Adoption Service.*[17] (See Notes, pages 117-119)

Groundbreaking ceremonies were held in May for the Thomas Higgins Memorial Building, for the offices of the fledgling adoption agency. Archbishop McIntyre dedicated the building on February 18, 1951.

Larry Stevens – Hollywood, CA

Former Holy Family and parking lot (now all parking lot)

Dedication of Thomas Higgins Memorial Building

Holy Family Adoption Service Thomas Higgins Memorial Building

The Citizens Adoption Committee was a very active group. Sister Mary Winifred was even requested by the committee to appear in Sacramento to explain to the Senate Social Welfare Committee that continuing aid to unborn children of needy mothers helped counteract black market adoptions. Sister Winifred testified in the Senate on March 30, 1952! Such was a high level of confidence and esteem at the state level placed in St. Anne's.[18] (See Notes, pages 119-122)

At the Assembly Interim Committee on Social Welfare (part of the Citizen's Adoption Committee), Sister Mary Winifred stated:

> To critics of this Aid program who charge that it promotes immorality: no normal girl or woman who has suffered the pangs of pregnancy out-of-wedlock would want to broadcast her predicament to others. To date I have never found an unmarried mother who personally knew or asked for Aid to Needy Children Assistance. My experience has taught me one thing, that bad girls do not have babies. They know the road to the abortion mills. It is the good girls who are unfortunate enough to become pregnant but courageous enough to see it through, that are our concern. Don't ever, ever think that an unmarried mother is immoral or unfit for society until you know all the facts. That girl may be your daughter, your niece, or your sister—she may be the innocent victim of an extremely difficult situation."[19] (See Notes, pages 119-122)

Sister Winifred with Sister Thomasine (Holy Family Adoption Service) with infant awaiting adoption

Steinart – Los Angeles, CA

The Franciscan Sisters withdrew from the operation of the agency in 1963 and the Sisters of Social Service assumed sponsorship of Holy Family Adoption Service.

A LETTER FROM A GRATEFUL ADOPTED CHILD

I am an out-of-wedlock child; born 30 years ago to a woman who became involved with a married man. He refused to divorce his wife and marry my mother. I was given for adoption; well-placed in a happy home. I grew up knowing I was adopted. I secretly despised my mother for allowing herself to become involved in such a sordid way. I waited until I was 28 to marry because I hated to divulge my own origin, fearing rejection. Today I wish I could see my mother and thank her for allowing me to live a normal life in a home with a mother AND father. I am sure I am not alone when I say as an adopted child, "Thank you, my wonderful Mother, wherever you may be, for your unselfishness. I shall be eternally grateful to you."

The child you gave up [21]

BEGINNINGS AT ST. ANNE'S

By Joyce Walter

Duglugolecki

I feel very blessed to have started my life's journey at St. Anne's Maternity Home in November of 1944. My birth mother made the difficult but loving choice that allowed me to become part of a wonderful family through adoption. After 30 days at St. Anne's, I was adopted. If I had had a chance to choose a set of parents myself, I could not have asked for better parents.

Nearly fifty years later, in the summer of 1994, I returned to St. Anne's as a volunteer in the childcare center. I had married my high school sweetheart, worked at the Los Angeles Times, raised two wonderful children, (we now have two beautiful grandchildren.), volunteered in their schools and in our community. In the years since my birth, St. Anne's Maternity Home had evolved with the changing times to meet the challenges of present day teens. The young women now in residence were single mothers raising their precious babies. Adoption was no longer the choice of the majority of teen mothers. Over the past 13 years, I have had the pleasure of being a volunteer and member of the St. Anne's Foundation Board of Trustees. I have observed the success of many of our young residents as they conquer the obstacles of being a single parent and become self-sufficient.

With the help of our outstanding management and experienced staff, St. Anne's has moved into the 21st century by providing for the mental health, education and physical needs of our young population. It has been exciting to be a part of this growth and even more exciting to think of the new challenges that we will face in the next 100 years. St. Anne's holds a very special place in my heart. It is the home of my earliest care and nurturing. Congratulations on 100 years of helping young women make loving choices.

In the 1950's, St. Anne's Foundation began to consider the next phase of expansion. The projects it envisioned were actually a response, "a humane answer to one of the greatest heartbreaks of present-day times: the growing number of babies being fed into what was termed the 'grey market,' and the terrorizing and victimizing of the unwed mother." It was estimated that there were 9,000 cases of unwed pregnancy in this state in 1953. There are only eight licensed maternity homes in California. The expansion would allow St. Anne's to double the amount of unwed mothers served. No self-respecting community can do less than take care of its children. "If young boys and girls are not taken care of in order to keep them out of trouble, then we have to pay the consequences. Unwed parenthood is one of these consequences."[22]

Rock-a-Bye Baby[23]
By Elaine Louise Gooley, Age 8

At Saint Anne's from far and near
Young girls enter sick with fear.
Some with shame and some alone,
Some are brought there straight from home.
Here a haven's found at last
To wipe the sorrow from the past.

Lovely Sisters give kind care
To the women that are there.
In this hospital they will stay
Till their babies come some day.
Healthy babies—pretty, too.
One of them could live with you!
From Sister Mary Winifred
You'll hear all that need be said
Of the details that you need
For a babe to clothe and feed
Some day I hope you'll get a child
But first you'll have to wait a while
In the meantime go to Sister Thomasine
Over at Holy Family
Whose work is love and charity.
For she will chose the one to be
The darling babe of your family.

During the 1950's, the girls at St. Anne's came from many different occupations, age groups, varied social and economic levels, and diverse religious groups. In 1952, St. Anne's served 403 girls and of those, 110 worked in clerical or secretarial positions, 26 were factory workers such as press operators and highly skilled technicians. There were also 19 graduate nurses and 9 in nurses' training, 18 waitresses, 15 sales clerks, 20 telephone operators, 5 cashiers, 1 model, 2 receptionists, a ballerina and women in other occupations such as artists and airline hostess.[24] (See Notes, page 122)

The expansion of St. Anne's in 1945-1946 was surpassed by an even greater growth and development of 1954-1955. Bishop Manning officiated at the groundbreaking on March 27, 1954. After many years of work, hope and prayers, and months of planning, the dream of a new improved facility began to dawn as a reality.

His Eminence James Francis Cardinal McIntyre blessed the new state of the art, fully accredited hospital on September 11, 1955. This was the fourth such ceremony since the Franciscan Sisters took charge of the Home in 1941.

Sister Winifred recalled the particulars:

1954 Groundbreaking –
Cardinal McIntyre, Sister Winifred and
Mrs. Fritz Burns

Costing $750,000, the new wing had two stories and a floor area of 32,000 sq feet. The hospital unit was complete with the delivery room suites, one surgical room for C-sections, sterilizers, supplies and clinical equipment. It also housed patients' rooms and five nurseries plus other amenities: consultation room, a visiting parlor, library, patients' sun parlor and a sun deck. The first floor (designated as the "prenatal" unit), had semiprivate rooms, complete with lavatory, toilet and closets. There was also a recreation room, visiting parlor, study rooms, library

Steinart – Los Angeles, CA

Artist's rendering – 1955 addition

Dedication 1955 building

and outdoor patio. The ground floor held the laundry, the boiler rooms and other service units. Study rooms were also on the ground floor. The existing buildings were used for treatment of out-patients, social service workers and administrative offices. How marvelous was this new addition![25]

Not only was the hospital expanded but the services provided to unwed mothers were enhanced. The changing times and the increasing social problem of unwed pregnancy demanded that more be done in way of comfort and to assist girls medically. By 1956, St. Anne's had a staff of eight Sisters in the convent, professional staff of 26, medical staff of 28 and another 35-40 volunteers in support of this great ministry. (See Notes, page 123)

The Tidings

CARDINAL JAMES FRANCIS A. MCINTYRE
ARCHBISHOP 1947–1952
CARDINAL 1952–1970

Just five years after the appointment of Archbishop McIntyre in 1947, Pope Pius XII raised him to the rank of cardinal, the first in the eastern United States. Cardinal McIntyre faced a period of incredible growth and expansion. Between 1948-1963, 82 parishes were added and Catholic schools in the Archdiocese tripled from 147-347, about one a month for 15 years. A tremendous wave of immigration brought an influx of Chinese, Japanese, Vietnamese, Koreans, and other Asiatic groups as there was also a rise of Hispanics and African Americans. In addition, this period also witnessed several upheavals within the Church—the Second Vatican Council and the exodus of many women religious from their communities.

GLADYS BURNS & ST. ANNE'S GUILD

By Frances Morehart

Roe Ann White Photography

Frances Morehart, Guild Member

In 1941, I was about sixteen when my mother, Gladys Burns, became involved with St. Anne's Maternity Hospital. Bishop Cantwell asked mother to get friends together to form a group, which later turned out to be the Guild. I worked in the nursery. How they would allow a sixteen year old girl to work in the nursery, I still don't know but I learned a lot.

Mother worked with Mrs. George (Peggy) Humphreys and so many ladies that were involved. They were wonderful—Mrs. Lorenzo Story, Mrs. Crockett, Mrs. Kaiser, and Peggy's mother were some of them. There was a party every Christmas at someone's home, then at the Beverly Club, I think the Ambassador Hotel, the Ebell Club, then down at St. Anne's in the patio. The annual bazaar would be held in the morning and a dinner in the evening that the husbands could attend.

Mother had been working at Santa Marta Clinic; she helped get that one started with my grandmother Scheller. My grandmother didn't do any of the actual work; she just donated, which was very nice of her. But Mom worked hard and I know she was down there a lot. Then when the Bishop asked her to do St. Anne's, she just went to the clinic one day a week and spent more time there because she liked that a lot better. I heard she scrubbed floors and she would just pitch in and help any where that she might be needed.

Several events were at our home. Mother loved that and so did my step-father, Fritz Burns. They were just party people and loved entertaining for charity. Saving babies was what captivated mother's interest similar to what we've done in Santa Barbara with Villa Majella. If you feel you've saved a few babies, it makes you very happy.

Gladys Burns

When I was married and had children, I had over 33 St. Anne's girls working for us—one at a time—until my son, Marty, was 13. And he asked, "Mom, how come everybody we have here is so fat?" And so I thought it was time that we got some regular help. I could not have raised my family without St. Anne's. These girls were so wonderful. And for many years afterwards I would hear from them. In fact, I was a matron of honor in several different weddings when they got married. They named their children after our children. We had a lot of wonderful things happen because of the girls that we had helping us. Today, I wish they could still do that because it's nice for the girls to see what a wholesome family is like and it helps them, too. I was very grateful they could stay with us even if it was just four or five months.

My step-father was very supportive of my mom in her work at St. Anne's. I make the lunch at the bazaar and we love doing it. I was in on the beginning of the Holy Family Adoption Agency auxiliary. Peggy Auth was the first president, I was the second president. We'd take the babies up to Queen of Angels for x-rays, etc. where there was a clinic and we'd help the doctors like Clyde Von der Ahe, John Reagan, and Bob Kelly. We'd do their leg work and just help out. We had a nice group of friends. When the adoption agency moved to Pasadena, I concluded my term on their board. But I was on the Board of the Guild and the Adoption Agency all together for over 27 years.

WAGE HOME PROGRAM

The Community Chest provided funds for St. Anne's but during WWII, funding had decreased, forcing us to find some creative ways to handle the shortage. Sister Mary Winifred asked members of her volunteer groups to take girls into their homes on a temporary basis during the last 4-6 months of the girls' pregnancies. This came to be known as the Wage Home Program: the unwed mother could live in the "wage home," perform certain domestic work and receive meals, a private room with bath, and a monthly salary from $60 to $100. The arrangement lightened the load at the facility and helped the pregnant teens and the families at the wage homes. This program functioned well into the sixties.[26]

THE FACE OF TEEN PREGNANCY IN THE 1950'S

From the start of St. Anne's in 1908, the unwed pregnant woman always struggled with hardships, social disgrace and condemnation. The 1950's were not much different.

When a girl finds that she is pregnant, she has mixed emotions—mainly fear and desperation. Frantically, she begins seeking help. Some girls are misguided and fall prey to the abortionist. One alternative is to place herself and her baby into the hands of private agents, but that can put her in peril. Some private agents mean well, others are out to make a fast buck. Another option is to seek shelter for safe delivery of her infant in a licensed, ethical and humane home.

With alarming frequency, in the 1950's and before, illegal abortions were being performed. At the time, the baby sales market had become a booming business, capitalizing on the financial gains at the expense of a defenseless infant.

For the unwed mother, a place like St. Anne's Maternity Hospital was really her best hope. Newspapers carried headlines that told the story:

"TRAFFIC IN HUMANS CITED BY KEFAUVER AT HEARING"
"MOTHER TELLS OF GIVING BABIES AWAY:
UNWED RELATE ADOPTION DETAILS AT KEFAUVER PROBE"
"CHARGE 200 ILLEGAL OPERATIONS"
"ANGUISHED MOTHER FORCED TO GIVE UP CHILD"
"GAVE AWAY TWIN BOYS"[27]

A 1957 issue of *St. Anne's Foundation Newsletter* cited an article on the issue of unwed pregnancy. The writer, W.H. Masters, supported the dilemma of unwed pregnancy. "The work of St. Anne's enfolds the pregnant girl with non-judgment, love, nurturing care and concern."[28]

In the copy of her written remarks addressed to St. Anne's Hospital Guild in 1957, Sister Winifred said:

Everyone loves success, accomplished alone or with others. It was Marie Dressler who said, and I quote, "Never one thing and seldom one person can make for a success. It takes a number of them merging into one perfect whole." This you have done! Success was inevitable because character is its real foundation, symbolized by the simple virtues you all possess, namely willingness, readiness, alertness, cooperation, patience, fortitude, and last but not least, your spirit of Christian charity.

It was Willis who said, "Gratitude is not only the memory but the homage of the heart, rendered to God for His goodness." Yes, indeed, gratitude to God makes the temporal blessings we at St. Anne's have received through your individual and collective efforts, a foretaste of Heaven. I want you to know that the Sisters, and particularly I, have a delicate appreciation of your goodness, your kindness, and your benevolence to us.

The peak reached in 1955 was something far beyond my fondest expectations. Back in 1941, St. Anne's was a very small hospital, 10 beds to be exact, an inadequate prenatal unit, clinic and no convent. Our first annual report read something like this: admissions 158; births 139; daily average in institution 15; clinic visits 553; per capita cost per day $1.00.

You have great generosity due to your concern and deep interest in our children who are becoming unwed mothers all too soon. You know our community as a whole does not look kindly upon our patients who have made such a mistake. They excuse almost anything else but unwed motherhood. So, one has been given insight and compassion to appreciate the utter hopelessness and terrible sorrow of the unwed mother. One must appreciate her great courage and strength to turn down the avenues of escape that are offered to her.... You give care for the unfortunate, you give hope and opportunity to the often homeless, and you are a silent bulwark that radiates warmth, strength and a hope for tomorrow to the patients of St. Anne's.

Today through the generosity of our devoted Guild members, the members—men and women—of our corollary St. Anne's Foundation, we have a wonderful new hospital, expanded clinic facilities, enlarged dormitory space, a lovely kitchen, modern laundry and plant. Our annual report gives us an entirely different picture than that just mentioned. Last year our admissions were 563; babies born 439; daily average in institution 71; clinic visits 4,072; per capita cost per day $7.15; age groups served 13-41 years; 129 of them were 17 years and under, with six at the tender age of 13.

Where the girls came from was a revelation to me: 308 came from Los Angeles County; 81 from other California counties; 126 from other states, and 13 from outside the United States: Philippine Islands, 1; Canada 2; Alaska 2; Honolulu, 3; Costa Rica 1; and Mexico 2. Ladies, we are truly a universal agency encompassing the whole world.[29]

In 1957, the outpatient clinic had 90 registered patients and it was the largest number at one time ever recorded in the clinic. These visits to the clinic allowed the unwed mothers residing outside of the institution the same access the residents have to medical and social services.

The broader picture showed a familiar trend that the number of out-of-wedlock births was still rising: 10,700 children of unwed pregnant mothers were born in California in 1956. About half of them (5,406) were born in Los Angeles County. That represents a birth every two hours of every day of the year! In 1940, 92 babies were born at St. Anne's. This had increased to 485 in 1957 but only 337 births were recorded in 1958. Even though St. Anne's may have been the largest hospital of its kind in the world, it did not handle even 10% of the out-of-wedlock births in Los Angeles County. In 1954, 63 girls 16 years of age or younger were hospitalized at St. Anne's. In 1957, 88 of the patients were under 16 years; 59 of the same age were recorded in 1958.[30]

A *Newsweek* article in 1958 gives us some comparative figures: "The sharp rise in the number of young unwed mothers in the U.S. is one of our most tragic and disturbing problems," says Katharine B. Oettinger, Chief of the Children's Bureau in Washington, DC. "In 1940, there were about 90,000 children born out-of-wedlock. During 1950, the figure was 141,000. This year [1958] it may reach 100,000. Two out of five of these births are to girls under 20, with nearly 5,000 cases a year to girls under 15."[31]

A survey was conducted of 329 girls, 16 years old or younger in the care of St. Anne's Maternity Hospital from January 1951 to December 1957. In this group, three were 12 year olds, twelve 13 year olds, and 45 were 14 year olds—60 girls were 14 years old or less. When these girls first became pregnant, they were 11, 12, and 13 years old. In the cases where the alleged father of the child is identified, experience indicated that the younger the girl, the more likely he was to be someone she knew, an uncle, brother, or step-father. Sad as it is, children of 11 have played with dolls at St. Anne's awaiting birth of their child.[32]

The care provided to the girls at St. Anne's was some of the highest caliber available. Dr. Clyde Von der Ahe reported on a survey of 329 girls 16 years of age and younger who were residents at St. Anne's from January 1951 to December 1957. Of these 329 girls, there were no miscarriages or premature births. Many teen births result in a low birth weight (LBW—defined as less than 5.5 pounds) but the babies born at St. Anne's had an average birth weight of 7.2 lbs. Even Cesarean Sections were relatively rare. Records revealed one C-Section in 1949. In fact, in a survey of 500 deliveries, records indicated only two. In over 5,000 girls who received care at the hospital, only one mother died.[33]

St. Anne's developed and achieved a respected position in the healthcare arena. The hospital was licensed by the State Department of Public Health and the State Department of Social Welfare. On the national level, the agency was fully accredited by the Joint Commission on Accreditation of Hospitals in the United States, a member of the National Conference of Catholic Charities, the Catholic Hospital Association of the United States and Canada, and the American Hospital Association.

CLINICAL RESEARCH

The progressive medical staff also conducted research projects that were in progress at St. Anne's, such as William G. Caldwell, M.D., chairman of the Clinical Research Committee, garnered two grants to further the efforts of the Clinical Research Committee. (See Notes, page 125-126)

Dr. Caldwell and his wife, Joan, were interviewed for a 1989 *Angel Messenger*. In 1949, Dr. Caldwell brought his date, actress Joan Leslie, to a Christmas Eve Mass. The Caldwell family had been associated with St. Anne's for some time. He did his residency in obstetrics and gynecology (OB-GYN) at Queen of Angels Hospital and residents were assigned to St. Anne's for their OB-GYN rotation.

The Caldwells in the late 1950's, pictured here at St. Anne's

"From the first moment I walked into St. Anne's," recalls Joan, "I became aware of the atmosphere—St. Anne's is a place of giving, of nurturing, of caring and understanding. I wanted to become a part of it, to help in any way I could." Dr. Caldwell's volunteer service helped to bestow upon St. Anne's an enduring quality reputation in the care provided to the pregnant teenagers.

The residency program at Queens of Angels was discontinued and until Medi-Cal began, St. Anne's was without medical assistance. But at the time, Dr. Caldwell and four colleagues stayed on to serve at St. Anne's. "We ran the entire clinic at no cost," said Dr. Caldwell, "and we were always there when we were needed, even though we had full practices of our own to tend. It was the same doctors, year in and year out. Sister Winifred called us 'her boys,' and we were. We were all like a family, the nuns and the doctors. And the amazing thing was that we never lost a girl. Each of us had that horrible experience in our private practices, where something terrible would happen to a woman in labor, but it never happened at St. Anne's. We used to talk about how remarkable that was, and I think we were blessed. I think maybe we got some extra help along the way."

Dr. Caldwell went on to serve as Chief of Staff for both St. Anne's Maternity Hospital and Queen of Angels Hospital. "Sister Winifred's warmth and direction kept us together. No one could have done what she did. She was incredibly intelligent and always a step ahead of everyone," said Dr. Caldwell. "There has always been warmth about St. Anne's," added Joan, "and even if you were there half the night assisting with some problem, you walked out feeling good."

"There's unspeakable joy about being part of something that is making a difference in the community," said Dr. Caldwell.[34]

Guilds and Auxiliaries

Over the years, since the St. Rose Guild provided initial support for St. Anne's, and the founding of St. Anne's Hospital Guild, many other support groups emerged either chartered by the Guild, Foundation, or hospital. The Guild records are well maintained although some of the other auxiliaries' support records no longer exist. But from the information that is available, the following organizations have supported the works of St. Anne's in different ways:

The first of these was the **Pilot Auxiliary**. This group was chartered at the Annual Spring Educational Meeting, Tuesday, June 11, 1957. It was the first auxiliary chartered by the Foundation and it worked with the Sisters and staff in a program of planned recreation and rehabilitation for the residents. Most of the members lived in Eagle Rock and suburban areas.

Sister Winifred Auxiliary, chartered September 19, 1957, was the second auxiliary to be formed to assist with fund raising and some of the medical care programs. Duty assignments included volunteers as dental assistants or work in the prenatal clinic, the trade training program, and the economy shop. Members primarily resided in the San Fernando Valley; it continued its existence into 2008.

The Westwood Auxiliary, also known as the **Helen Clark Auxiliary,** was chartered by the Foundation on November 13, 1958. Most of the members were from the Westwood area and Mrs. Adolphe L. Flynn was the first president. The purpose of the Auxiliary was to "help administer, improve and implement the rehabilitation program for residents and to support fund raising efforts of the St. Anne's Foundation."

Mabel Mosler Auxiliary was established in about 1962 (some reference 1965) by the Guild and is still functioning as an active auxiliary as of 2008, assisting with fundraising efforts and the Bazaar.

Wage Home Auxiliary, formally chartered in March 1958, supported the supervised work of the wage home program. Mrs. Richard E. Giles, the founding president and auxiliary members assisted the girls being assigned to the private homes.

Las Anitas Service (Little Anne's), part of the administrative and social service functions of St. Anne's, was formed in 1959 and replaced the name of the Wage Home Auxiliary. Mrs. Richard Giles was the founding president of the Service.

Gladys Burns Auxiliary was chartered by the Foundation about 1965 and the members were located primarily in Hermosa Beach. It was named for one of the founding members of the Guild and strong supporter, Gladys Burns. Their role supported the bazaar, fundraising and service at St. Anne's.

Josephine Brant Auxiliary was chartered in 1963 with Mrs. Roy Ellender, founding president. Members of the auxiliary resided in West Valley. Mrs. Thomas J. Brant (Josephine) had long been a donor to St. Anne's but felt she should do something to help poor girls establish themselves to make a living. In 1961, the Josephine Brant Scholarship Fund came into existence.

Juniors of St. Anne's Hospital Guild was founded in 1960 and their projects included recreational and educational activities for the patients of the hospital as well as sponsorship of a booth at the annual Guild Christmas bazaar. An adjunct to the Juniors was an auxiliary of teenage daughter-and-mother teams called the **Cherubs of St. Anne's Hospital.**

Loretta Young Auxiliary was established in honor of Mrs. Loretta Young Lewis who was president of the Foundation from

1947-1952. The group became the fourth Auxiliary affiliated with the Foundation, approved at the September 14, 1961 meeting.

Joachim League, founded in 1968, was a group of men who wanted to help in the work being done to assist young unmarried pregnant women who were pregnant and wanted to have their babies.

Rony League, founded in 1989 for young adults between 21-40 years of age, assisted with various activities with the residents.

Orange County Guild of St. Anne's Hospital was created about 1972; by 1987 it supported St. Anne's by its annual "Day at the Races."

Ventura County Guild of St. Anne's Hospital, founded in 1971, existed prior to the establishment of outreach services in that locale. Once the outreach services were discontinued, the Guild's connection with St. Anne's ceased.

An auxiliary known as Professional Women's Auxiliary (PWA) was established around 1987. Another was the ISATT group, founded in 1980 from St. Jude's Catholic Church in Westlake, comprised totally of the 10 a.m. choir members (hence the "I Sing At The Ten). They provided support to St. Anne's Community Outreach program in Ventura County.

Two other organizations connected with outreach services were Friends of Gateway in Pomona (formed in 1972) and Friends of Villa Majella in Santa Barbara (organized in 1985) to serve the young women in these two locales.

Coordinating Council. Sister Winifred created this body from leadership in the Foundation and all of the volunteer organizations affiliated with St. Anne's Maternity Hospital. The purpose of the council was to act as a steering committee to coordinate all women's activities; to act as a clearing committee to compile a master calendar of events and disseminate information on the activities and projects of all the groups; to serve in an advisory capacity, giving direction where needed; and to stimulate ways and means of uniting the efforts of all in support of the Guild's annual Christmas Bazaar.

Over the years, these groups and others were the means of support and for many young women and their children without whom St. Anne's would not have flourished.

Throughout St. Anne's history, young girls have shared their amazing stories of survival. Here is one story by Miss Maureen Connor, which was printed in an issue of the *Foundation Newsletter*:

ANITA'S STORY

Anita arrived at St. Anne's without an appointment one afternoon in the summer of 1961. She was a neatly dressed, attractive, slender girl with an extremely shy, diffident and uncertain personality. Although she was 20 years of age, her whole demeanor was that of a much younger girl, and from talking with her, one had the impression of a lost fawn-like creature terrified of her situation, mutely asking for guidance and help. Anita was unmarried, already five months pregnant, and had learned about St. Anne's from a doctor months previously. It had taken considerable courage on her part and not a little desperation to prompt her to seek the help she was told she would find at St. Anne's. Even now she was uncertain of how she would be received due to the tremendous guilt feelings which her out-of-wedlock pregnancy caused her.

Midway in a family of ten, Anita grew up in an atmosphere of real poverty and hardship where hunger was often a daily occurrence. There was discord, too, occasioned by an alcoholic father and a harassed mother often unable to meet the demands of her unfortunate children. The father was a pathetic, feckless figure who found it impossible to hold a job and sought escape and solace in drink whenever possible. Anita had little respect for her father and mother and although full of compassion for her mother, left home when she was 16 without completing high school.

Without even the benefit of a close relationship with her older siblings, Anita led an aimless life finding what employment she could and living in a cheap apartment on her own. Lonely and insecure, she became involved with a gay philanderer who was himself without roots and who had no intention of marriage—as she bitterly learned when she told him of her pregnancy. Rejected by the father of her child, reluctant to return home and present her already dispirited mother with an added burden, Anita had tardily arrived at St. Anne's.

Anita was carefully placed in a wage home where she was accepted and respected as an individual. She continued to attend St. Anne's as an outpatient and as her pregnancy progressed.

She became more aware of her own needs and was able to be more objective and tolerant of her father, coupled with a more supportive attitude toward her mother who by this time was aware of the pregnancy. Anita regained her self-esteem and with it, a realistic acceptance of herself and her limitations and was able to plan more constructively for her baby and for her own future.

"The wage-home family took a personal interest in her and although by no means controlling, displayed concern for her future. The wage home family suggested that Anita continue to live with them for an indefinite period following delivery, offering her a substantial salary increase and the opportunity to complete her high school education. She found the fortitude and courage to finalize her plans for adoption, secure in the knowledge that worthy parents were waiting to welcome her child into their hearts and that it would grow up fully aware of the sacrifice she was now making to safeguard its future happiness. When Anita attended her postnatal check-up six weeks after delivery, she was smiling and confident, presenting a marked contrast to that shy frightened girl who had come to St. Anne's."[35]

A Thank You Letter

Dear Sister Winifred,

I should not have waited so long to let you know how much I appreciated all St. Anne's did for me. I finally find the time to write in gratitude and thankfulness to you and to all the other Sisters, the social workers, the volunteers in the auxiliaries—all of whom do so much for girls like myself. St. Anne's means much to a girl in trouble. It is a shelter from the storm of abuses and shame a young girl in trouble would have to face at home. At St. Anne's, you are not treated like a criminal or something dirty that has done wrong and must be punished. The girls are treated kindly and all their needs are taken into consideration. You grow to bear the burden of the situation you have gotten yourself into and you face up to reality. You start rebuilding your life.... I will always appreciate and be grateful to you and the others who made it possible for me to go to St. Anne's and still be able to continue on and make something of my life.

Respectfully yours, S.S. [36]

The educational program enjoyed the support of several outside agencies. One, for example, provided grants in aid to help the girls initiate or continue their business or professional education on any academic level and at the school of their choice.

Dee Dickson, Club Editor of the *Los Angeles Herald Express*, wrote:

> A young miss today fingers a scholarship certificate in the pocket of her maternity smock and knows that because there are people who care she may someday realize her professional dream. She is not aware, as she sits at St. Anne's that she will face many trials and adjustments before and after the birth of her expected child. But now she can contemplate a future. Now she has another chance. Maybe she will still be able to become an electronics engineer. Her morale has lifted noticeably since the day when Exec Business and Professional Women of Los Angeles selected her as their winner of the club's scholarship grant.[37]

CHAPLAINS

Since the 1940's, the Order of Friars Minor provided chaplaincy services to St. Anne's. Before coming to St. Anne's, Fr. Donald Gander, O.F.M. had been in parish work at St. Joseph's in Los Angeles and chaplain at Queen of Angels Hospital. Other chaplains for St. Anne's were Father Julius Gliebe, O.F.M. 1949-1951 and Father Juniper Doolin, O.F.M., who came from Old Mission Santa Barbara, appointed chaplain in 1951.

Father Herbert Patterson, Chaplain 1962-1996

Father Herbert Patterson, O.F.M., first came to St. Anne's in 1962 after his assignment at a Long Beach parish. Father Herbert served as chaplain from 1962-1996, the longest tenure of chaplains assigned to St. Anne's. He was friend and spiritual counselor to generations of young women who lived with us during their pregnancies. Father Herbert died on November 18, 1997 at the age of 88.

Father William Brand was assigned to St. Anne's in 1996 and left in 2002. He worked in the youth ministry services with the residents.

UNITED WAY, INC. OF LOS ANGELES COUNTY

The agency organized into a single campaign combining 29 separate Community Chests and United Fund, embraced 155 communities and nearly 300 voluntary health and welfare services. St. Anne's Maternity Hospital became an agency partner when, in 1925, it was a founding agency of the Los Angeles Welfare Federation, Inc., also known as the Los Angeles Area Community Chest. The new unified organization was the means to provide everyone the opportunity to give where they work for services where they live. Moreover, the new county-wide organization potentially could raise more money for needed services and provide full accountability to the contributing public that wants to know where, how and why funds are spent. United Way, Inc. is the culmination of years of effort on the part of leaders in county communities. St. Anne's was pleased to be a partner in the launching of this single, combined, county-wide annual appeal. [38]

1960's EXPANSION

In 1962, St. Anne's proposed plans for expansion included an Educational Center, Medical Center and multipurpose auditorium. The Social Need and Desirability Study at St. Anne's (circa 1962), projected growth of St. Anne's because the rationale for the needed facilities was a waiting list of 57 girls. There was a rapidly accelerating, continued trend of out-of-wedlock births occurring in all age groups and from all socio-economic levels of society.

Educational Center

A new educational center was essential. The old classrooms were poorly located, inadequate and overcrowded. Senior students used the patients' dining room as a make-shift classroom. The Vocational Training School was in a basement room in the 1930 wing. Vocational training needed to add courses for rehabilitation. (See Notes, pages 126-128)

His Excellency, the Most Reverend John J. Ward, J.C.L, D.D., Auxiliary Bishop of Los Angeles, officiated at groundbreaking ceremonies on January 5, 1964. (See Notes, pages 126-128)

The education center was completed in just nine months. The dedication was held on Sunday, October 4, 1964, the feast of St. Francis with Bishop John J. Ward officiating. The center was named for Harold and Fern McAlister in honor of their

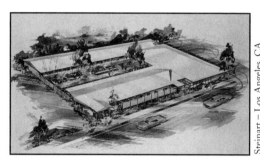

Artist's Rendering – 1964 Educational Center

Steinart – Los Angeles, CA

Educational Center Classroom – 1964

Rothschild Photo – Los Angeles, CA

Harold and Fern McAlister
Donors of the Educational Center

devotion and generosity to unfortunate children in the community. (See Notes, pages 126-128)

Rothschild Photo – Los Angeles, CA

Educational Center Homemaking Room – 1964

The Board of Directors for AID United Givers honored Sister Mary Winifred Falker and was recognized in 1964 for her work at St. Anne's with the "Humanitarian of the Year Award." Charles R. Fleishman, President of the Board, said, "I know of no year when we have had a recipient to equal this year's in dedicated service, length of service, and scope of service." The criterion for the award required the recipient to have made a significant medical discovery or been engaged in continued humanitarian activities far above the norm.

Sister Winifred said with her characteristic wit and humor:

From you only, as a friend of long standing, would I permit such flattery! But your reference to "far above norm" in the criteria for this word has me worried; not for myself but for the recipient next year. Who is this Norm? This award honors equally my fellow Sisters, who pioneered with me in this work of caring for society's outcasts, the unwed mothers. It honors our dedicated staff members. It recognizes the significant contribution made by our devoted staff of physicians and dentists who donate their services to our patients. But not least, you have honored hundreds of men and women who, in volunteering their time and talent, have played such a significant part in developing St. Anne's physical plant as a unique setting for our varied programs of superior medical care and our educational and rehabilitative program for teenage unwed mothers. Most significantly, to me, this award indicates public acceptance and appreciation for the work St. Anne's Maternity Hospital is rendering this community.[39]

It is truly a legacy of love.

Medical Unit

The next project at St. Anne's was to construct the 23,000 square-foot, three-level medical unit by general contractors D.W. McNeil Co., Inc. Groundbreaking for the medical unit wing occurred on November 11, 1964. Twenty-one new beds were needed to accommodate the waiting list. The peripheral cottages had been torn down which made the need for additional beds even more essential and because the present facilities for medical care and social service counseling were inadequate and obsolete—lacking waiting-room areas and conference areas, restroom facilities, casework offices, treatment and consultation rooms. Facilities for the X-Ray Department, Dental Clinic and Clinical Laboratory were cramped and makeshift. The services were fragmented and spread out, creating physical hardship and unavoidable staff inefficiency.

The cost of this project was approximately $1 million plus another $100,000 for capital equipment and furnishings. It had been kept a well-guarded secret until the name of the new addition as announced: "The Sister Mary Winifred Clinic and Social Service Wing." James Francis Cardinal McIntyre officiated at the dedication which was held on the Feast of St. Anne, July 26, 1968. Cardinal McIntyre said, "This charity is an affair of the heart. As I look about me, I see the same warm, kind faces of friends and supporters, year after year helping Sister Winifred doing this marvelous work. The Holy Father took note of the excellent work performed at St. Anne's in a quiet, humble and affectionate way, supported by a wonderful group of people, and in the appreciation of his heart, and his generosity, he has penned his signature to his own picture and I am

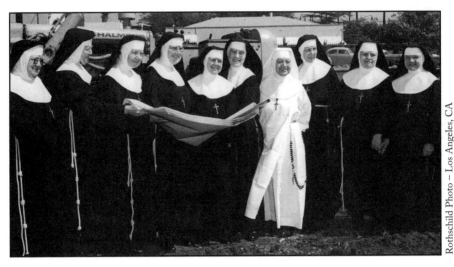

Rothschild Photo – Los Angeles, CA

Franciscan Sisters plan for new unit – 1966:
Sister Borromea Feier, Sister Mary Casimir Makstutis, Sister Rosalia Fueglister,
Sister Timothy Marie Flaherty (General Superior), Sister Winifred Falker,
Sister Agreda Leahy, Sister Carmelita Dominguez, Sister Joan Miller,
Sister Elaine Grochowski and Sister Joanita Grochowski

commissioned to present Sister Winifred this Blessing of our Holy Father."[40]

The 1965 operating budget was $457,166. That year 1,069 girls were accepted for care in the social service department; another 1,136 were referred to other agencies. The hospital had a total of 912 patients. Bed occupancy was at 93.6%, indicating a full prenatal unit at all times plus a waiting list averaging 70 apprehensive girls each month. A total of 725 babies were delivered to 718 mothers, and some even included seven sets of twins. Eighteen Caesarean-sections were performed in 1966 as compared to 9 in 1965, but all were seriously complicated cases. An all time high of 603 (83.5%) were relinquished for adoption. In September, hospital occupancy reached a new high—104 patients.[41]

Early chronicles and publications refer to the existence of two nurses from the St. Rose Guild who provided voluntary service during

St. Anne's early years. In 1962, Sister Winifred mentioned in her speech a founding nurse, still living at age 96. A photo of a Miss Donnelly pictured in this book is probably the nurse. However, from an article in a Los Angeles paper neither dated nor identified, announces the death of one of the founding nurses, Mary Frances McDonald: "Now and then, in the swift procession of human events, there passes a rare and beautiful soul whose complete self-effacement and whole-hearted devotion to some charity makes us pause gladly to pay a tribute that

Dedication of Sister Mary Winifred Clinic & Social Service Wing – 1968

neither great wealth nor high social standing alone could secure. Such a one was Miss Mary Frances McDonald.... Her exemplary life has left its impress on the life of many a child whom fate brought to her hospitable door and her memory will ever be fondly cherished by all who knew her, and she would not wish for better monument. Her work at St. Anne's, along with her friend, Miss Donnelly, lasted for many years and without money. The heritage of St. Anne's owes a debt of gratitude to these selfless women who gave without counting the cost."

On October 29, 1966, a symposium, the first of its kind in the United States, on the "Medical Management of Unwed Mothers," was sponsored by St. Anne's Medical Staff. The concept for the project was originated by Clyde Von der Ahe, Chief of Staff. The event included nationally recognized speakers and received a resolution of commendation from the Board of Directors of St. Anne's. The commendation was a way of acknowledging the work of the medical staff and to demonstrate appreciation for their outstanding efforts. The effect of this symposium and the distribution of the four papers presented had lasting and impact in obtaining national recognition of the work and services of St. Anne's.

A HEALING MINISTRY

By Clyde Von der Ahe, MD

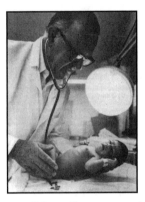

I became involved at St. Anne's in June 1946, when I returned from three years of service overseas in the Army Medical Corps. It was then that we began the residency program at Queen of Angels. Bob Kelly, Bill Caldwell and I were chosen as the first three residents in obstetrics and gynecology. We were assigned to deliver for the girls at St. Anne's as part of the residency program.

My colleagues and I were instrumental in conducting the prenatal exams and Sister Madeleine was the nun in charge of the clinic at St. Anne's. We also had A.M. McCarthy, Tom O'Neill, and Kathleen R. Harrington as attending physicians.

When I was still a resident, about 1949, I was not yet married. One of the other residents had four tickets and invited me to an event in the community. During the evening, there was a drawing and I won a television set. Now, this was when TVs were first coming out. I went home, said to my mom and sister, "The girl we were with wants me to give the TV back to the actress who paid for the tickets." They decided that was not a good idea. Of course I didn't give it back, so I just donated it to the nuns at St. Anne's. Not long after that, I had an urgent call from Sr. Madeleine, which usually meant there was a delivery to do. She met me at the door and said, "Will you come in and tune the TV for us?!"

My mother, who was involved in many things, had a great interest in St. Anne's and was part of the Guild when Sister Winifred was there.

Through the years, as the census grew at the facility, we were delivering 100 babies a month, which I thought was pretty good! Following the completion of our residency, Bob Kelly and I went on to the staff at St. Anne's, where we started training other residents.

When the new hospital was built, we put in our own Cesarean-section room, which was a big step. Prior to that, a girl needing a C-section had to go to Queens. Eventually, I became Chief of Staff as did Bill Caldwell. There was another Kelly, Jim, who was still in the Navy when his brother and I got started at St. Anne's, and he came on board later.

One time when Tom O'Neil was examining a girl, he was subjected to the girl's sister jabbering away incessantly. She said to O'Neil, "My sister says I'm crazy." As Tom walked out of the room, he said with exasperation, "I think she's right!"

Another evening I went over to help a resident with a C-section. Ken Olsen, who was a meat cutter at Vons and for St. Anne's, met me. He asked if he could watch. I told him that he could and I put him in a cap and gown and brought him in. I said to the resident, "This is 'Dr.' Olsen, he's going to observe." Not fooled at all, Joe Marco, looked up and said, "Hi, Ken", to which 'Dr.' Olsen said, "Hi, Joe…!"

When I was applying for entrance into the elite Pacific Coast Obstetrical and Gynecological Society, a requirement for entrance was to do a paper that was acceptable to the society and suitable for publication. My paper, initially entitled "Heavenly Footprints" was on teenage pregnancy. *The American Journal of Obstetrics and Gynecology* felt it wasn't scientific enough, so it was changed. The American College of Obstetricians and Gynecologist (ACOG) held the position that teenage pregnancy was a high-risk pregnancy. My premise was that if these teens received adequate prenatal care and obstetrical services, they would do as well as, if not better, than older pregnant women.

About Sister Winifred; I loved that woman. She was only five-foot-four, but all dynamite! Once she needed to have some surgery done and she asked me to do it and I told her I thought she might want someone with more experience. "No," she said, "I want you!"

Another time, we had just admitted a girl into St. Anne's, who arrived with a letter from a San Francisco physician, explaining why she was sent. "Please be advised that there were no less than 15 attempts to abort this woman. Abort her!" I can't quote what we said in the letter that we wanted to send him. We told the girl, "We are just going to deliver you." She said, "All I wanted was my baby."

When Sr. Winifred called one of us, even if we were busy with patients, she'd say, "Come NOW," and we did.

We got the idea of having seminars on the unwed mothers and did so for several years while I was Chief of Staff and a little beyond that. We came up with a paper on unwed pregnancy, the relationship with the parents, the father of the baby, and we had somebody from Santa Monica who checked it out and later published it. Requests for reprints came in from all over the world; well, at least as far away as Australia.

I had a wonderful respect for Sr. Winifred and that kept me at St. Anne's. Then they put me on the board when Sr. Margaret Anne was the chairman. Now, I'm retired and in 2008 I will be 90! While on the Board, I was made Program Chairman, reviewing the program, incidents like the girls going AWOL. Every month there were some; admission and discharges were about equal.

Many years later, it was finally decided to honor me but I was unhappy about that since so many others who were my mentors, came before me. So in 1990, I finally accepted the honor in the name of all those who preceded me.

In September 1967, a joint decision was made to continue the affiliation of both Queen of Angels Hospital and St. Anne's in the residency teaching program, beginning October 1, 1967 on a full-time rotating basis for all residents. Approval was sought in August 1968, for the use of St. Anne's Maternity Hospital by students of Queen of Angels School of Nursing as a teaching adjunct. Children's Hospital was also affiliated with St. Anne's Maternity Hospital for pediatric residency.

St. Anne's authorities were rightfully disturbed by a 1968 Medi-Cal ruling that no more than three days' postpartum care in normal cases was deemed medically necessary. Medi-Cal is California's version of medical insurance for the indigent. The ruling declared that the additional days were purely for social reasons. St. Anne's medical staff and Blue Cross became embroiled in controversy until the conflict was settled in favor of the hospital, allowing a five-day stay for normal post-partum cases. In the early 1970's, however, the three day stay became mandatory.

A memo was received in December 1968, from the California Hospital Association indicating that two new laws pertaining to consent by minors had become effective November 13, 1968: 1) Minors of age 15 years and over may consent to medical, surgical, dental or hospital treatment without parental approval, provided the minor is living, even temporarily, apart from parents or guardian and provided that the minor manages his own financial affairs, regardless of whether or not he is financially independent; 2) Minors 12 years of age or over may personally consent to medical, surgical or hospital treatment without parental approval, provided the treatment is for communicable diseases. Under both laws the parents or guardian may be notified about the pending medical care, but such notice is not required.

Parental or guardian permission was recommended when it could be obtained without undue inconvenience, for precautionary reasons, even though such a parent or guardian had no right to prevent the minor from receiving care authorized by these laws. Although a parent or guardian might become liable for bills incurred by minors described in both laws, either by agreeing to pay the bill or by authorizing the care, a parent or guardian could not be held responsible for payment of bills incurred by minors who had been treated solely upon their own consent under each law.

Tom Owenson joined St. Anne's as a new administrative assistant to Sister Winifred. He was the former commanding officer of a naval seaport ship, the *USS Mercer* that included a 40-bed hospital.

In her last speech before St. Anne's Foundation, Sister Winifred said that 515 girls relinquished their babies for adoption and 234 kept their babies. She pointed out that increasingly, girls kept their babies. Society was becoming more accepting of the unwed mother and her infant. The stigma that once prevailed seemed to be vanishing.

DEATH OF SISTER MARY WINIFRED

Sister Mary Winifred Falker died on July 23, 1970 at the age of 75. She was professed as a Franciscan Sister of the Sacred Heart for 53 years. Her memorable service at St. Anne's left a lasting legacy. By the time of her death, Sister Mary Winifred saw St. Anne's grow from a 10-bed facility to a hospital encompassing more than an entire city block with a capacity of 90 prenatal beds, modern clinic facilities and social service quarters that served over 1,000 young women annually. Tributes to Sister Winifred abounded; one came from the *Herald Examiner* in Los Angeles:

When she came to Los Angeles in 1941, St. Anne's Hospital for Unwed Mothers was a little, stucco, one-story building nearly hidden by a worn out looking hedge. It had room for only 12 persons. Sister Mary Winifred, the hospital's administrator for 29 years, would never tell you her part in the hospital's growth. What she would tell you was, "St. Anne's is what it always was: a refuge, a way station, amid public stigma and private grief."

She had a lot to learn when she arrived here, a registered nurse, with many years behind her in top administrative posts in large, modern hospitals in Chicago and Santa Barbara. "I was pretty naïve about unwed mothers when I was first sent here," she said once. "I guess I looked upon them much the same way as society did then—the girl was a no-gooder; a bad girl. Once in a great while I had seen them before in the big, general hospitals where I was, but everything about them seem so secretive. When I came here, I had no idea, no understanding at all of the work to be done. I was absolutely grass-green. There are no bad girls here," she said quietly, "only sad and forsaken ones. They are so loveable, not bad, not anything like bad...."

There was a lot of work to be done at St. Anne's when the tiny Franciscan arrived here. There were the needed material improvements so very obvious to the trained eye—and there were the needed immaterial improvements that even the trained eye had to learn to "see."

She learned.[42]

Sister was lovingly laid to rest on the Feast of St. Anne, July 26th. Her ability to use her gifts and talents for the good of the institution dedicated to St. Anne stands as a testimony to her determination. Comments on Sister's death are excerpts from the hospital newsletter: [43]

...Lady of God...We have sustained a loss but we have an advocate in Heaven.

—James Francis Cardinal McIntyre, Archbishop of Los Angeles

...I think any of us who have been part of St. Anne's will feel that while the teacher has left us for awhile, the instruction, example and love we have all known through Sister Winifred will never be forgotten....

—William R. Howell, Senior Vice President, Union Bank and Trust
Company and former President of St. Anne's Foundation

...She built from her dreams. I am reminded of the line of a poem which states, 'The Dreamer dies but never dies the Dream.' She has left bricks and mortar—a program to be proud of but more a dream which will never die....

—Brigadier Gwen Carruthers,
Administrator, Booth Memorial Hospital

I read abut the death of Sister Winifred and I want you to know that I was terribly sorry to hear such sad news.... I left St. Anne's six months ago and my baby wasn't adopted until yesterday.... But thanks to the grace of God and a lot of prayers from many people, my son now has a promising future in a home full of love.... Thank you for everything. I'll never forget you. I've enclosed $2.00. Would you please have Father Herbert say a Mass for Sister Winifred and one also in thanksgiving for my son, Phillip's adoption...?

—A former patient

LORETTA YOUNG REMINISCES

As Told to Share Fay Koch
(From St. Anne's Angel Messenger, 1970, Volume 4, Number 3)

Sister Mary Winifred was diagnosed with leukemia. Loretta Young had a terrible time dealing with this. She shared these thoughts after Sister Winifred's funeral:

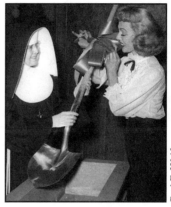

Sister Winifred and
Loretta Young

"I got my first shock about Sister Winifred and her life and death struggle with leukemia about two years ago. I waited until I thought I had calmed down emotionally before I phoned her. But when she got on the phone, I burst into tears. She said, 'Never mind, dear, God knows what He is doing. So whatever it is, and whatever He has in store for us, is what we want, ISN'T IT?'

"Of course this was always her attitude. I saw this woman live a life of abandonment to God's will. She always said to me, 'Everything is providential, Loretta. The only trick we have to do is to find out what He wants—find out His will for us. I have found that His will for me is what happens to me.'

"Sister was a reasonable kind of woman. She never expected more from a person than he could give. She never expected more of the board members, the nurses, the girls, the unmarried fathers—than each one could give. She always treated a person as an individual with his own capacity. Some of us are thimbles full. Some of us are gallons. She never pressed beyond the individual's capacity to give. Most people with dreams, you know, scare you to death because they're often so unrealistic. Not Sister.

Paul E. Wolfe

Loretta Young and Sister Winifred

"I've worked with some brilliant executives in all the studios and in large organizations. I've never met an executive like Sister Winifred. She was God oriented. She ran everything with the help of God's gentle hand. Sister usually got what she wanted. But she never pushed. For two years I had been saying, 'No, I don't want to accept the presidency of the Foundation Board, because I'm an actress and I don't know anything about it. I'll just write you a check if I can afford it, because I don't know anything about charity work.'

"She was always charming about it, but while I was in Europe I received a cable from her. It said, 'Imperative that you accept presidency of Foundation. Will explain when you come home.' I cabled back 'ok' and when I got home, of course, I tore down there and said, 'Well, what's imperative?' She said, 'We need you. That's what's imperative. And the reason we need you is because I feel really that you need us even more. Because when you're getting to the point in life when you consider charity a check, a tax deduction, you're on the wrong track, Loretta. We'll get the advantage of it, but you won't get anything out of it. And unless you have a person-to-person contact and you really give of yourself—not of your excess cash—you're going to miss the whole point.' It didn't take me long to find out how right she was."

Part Three

ST. ANNE'S IN TRANSITION
1970's-2000's

The past 30 years have seen dramatic changes in our society, and St. Anne's has changed with them. With profoundly different attitudes toward sexuality, marriage and childbirth out-of-wedlock, coupled with radically different healthcare delivery and payment systems, traditional maternity homes have become a thing of the past. In 1976, St. Anne's closed its hospital wing, and since the early years of the 1980's St. Anne's focus had increasingly moved to serving the diverse needs of indigent, abused and neglected adolescent girls and their babies, during the teens' pregnancies and the first years of their babies' lives.

After Sister Winifred's death, the board appointed Mrs. Robert Coyne as the Administrator, a position she held for two years. In 1972, Tom Owenson was named Administrator of St. Anne's, providing St. Anne's with outstanding leadership for the next 30 years.

Duglugolecki

AT THE HELM
By Tom Owenson

I'm pleased to have this opportunity to congratulate St. Anne's on the 100th anniversary of its founding. St. Anne's has always been successful because of the many talented and committed volunteers it has attracted. Thanks to them, St. Anne's flourished for decades before there was any government payment for the services provided to unmarried pregnant young women.

I started working at St. Anne's in August, 1969 as the Administrative Assistant to Sister Mary Winifred Falker, OSF, who was Administrator from 1941 to 1970. The Franciscan Sisters of the Sacred Heart had taken over St. Anne's from the Catholic Welfare Bureau in that year, and Sister Winifred brought the skills and foresight that enabled the organization to grow enormously during her tenure. Sister Winifred was a true renaissance woman who, as I recall, had all the credentials to conduct a hospital single-handedly. She was a Registered Nurse, Nurse Anesthetist, Registered Medical Record Librarian, and licensed Laboratory Technician; all skills needed in any hospital. But her talents went far beyond mere credentials. She was most significantly a charismatic person of extreme energy who drew people into the small, almost anonymous organization. In 1941, St. Anne's was a small maternity hospital of about 6 beds and with a residence for only about 10 girls. There was also a program which placed girls in volunteers' homes during their pregnancies. Sister Winifred built St. Anne's into a 90-bed residence and a 21-bed licensed and accredited hospital, widely known and respected as a major contributor to the social welfare network in Southern California.

As I began my experience, St. Anne's was viewed primarily as a hospital, and it was organized in that model. There was an active and supporting medical staff—mostly physicians who worked primarily at Queen of Angels Hospital, which was also run by the Franciscan Sisters of the Sacred Heart. There was the full complement of nurses needed to operate the hospital 24 hours a day, seven days a week; and there were all of the supporting staff needed to run a hospital, which included accounting, administration, plant operation, human resources, food service, laundry, purchasing, and housekeeping. The residence was served primarily by the Social Services Department, and there wasn't a single person overseeing the residence at night. Of course, the Sisters lived in the building and could be called upon if there was need. At the time, there were more than a dozen Sisters in residence at St. Anne's, many retired but always available. Typically, if a resident had a problem in the evening, she would go up to the hospital floor where one of the on-duty nurses would take care of her or call Sister Winifred.

The hospital was a very busy place at this time. In 1969 there were over 1,000 births in our 21-bed hospital. At that time, delivered mothers remained hospitalized for 5 days after giving birth. About half of the babies were put up for adoption, and they usually remained in the nursery for two weeks or more.

By 1970 we had added night staffing for the residence, but this was initially only one person. The residents in those days were a fairly docile group of girls who appreciated the opportunity they were being given to live at St. Anne's, and there were few incidents of misbehavior. I do recall that Sister Winifred had me patrolling around the outside of the residence each morning to look for footprints under the windows!

After Sister Winifred's death, Mrs. Robert Coyne was named Administrator, and I was promoted to Assistant Administrator. During that period there were some significant events. In May 1971, the Franciscan Sisters leased the operation of Queen of Angels Hospital to an investor-owned hospital-operating-corporation. However, they retained control of the Queen of Angels School of Nursing and Queen of Angels Clinic. I was given the additional responsibility of being the Director until further decisions were made about the clinic's future. That additional job lasted until May 1972, when Mrs. Coyne left St. Anne's and I was named Administrator. The San Fernando earthquake had occurred in February 1971, and resulted in a lot of superficial damage to St. Anne's new residence building. While the structure was not compromised, the ceiling tiles and framework fell down in many rooms, plaster interior walls were cracked, and the exterior stucco was damaged. The quake, occurring at 6 a.m., panicked the residents. Father Herbert Patterson, the resident chaplain, and the Sisters, quickly herded the girls into the Chapel for an impromptu Mass, after which they settled down and assisted in cleaning up the residence.

Eight months after I was named Administrator of St. Anne's, the U.S. Supreme Court upheld the case of Roe v. Wade. This decision effectively resulted in abortion being an alternative to having a baby out-of-wedlock. In California at that time, pregnant minors were deemed eligible for Medi-Cal based on their own lack of assets rather than their parents', so girls could get abortions without cost or parental consent or knowledge. It was anticipated that there would be a substantial decrease in number of girls seeking to have their babies in maternity homes and then place the children for adoption. Facing this concern, the Director of Public Relations, Tom Gilliam, suggested that St. Anne's begin an aggressive ad campaign to make teenagers aware of our services. Prior to this time, St. Anne's was not well known outside the Catholic community, and advertising our services to attract clients was an innovative and controversial move. Given the go-ahead, Mr. Gilliam became actively involved in the Public Relations Society, and saturated the airwaves with public service announcements about St. Anne's services. The result was that we continued to have a "full house" up to the 1990's.

St. Anne's had a dual corporate structure at this time. The Maternity Hospital was conducted by the Franciscan Sisters of the Sacred Heart, and all members of the Board of Directors were Sisters. St. Anne's Foundation was a separate organization, staffed by Tom Gilliam and Marye Kimoto. Sister Winifred actively involved local leaders in the mission of St. Anne's. Many of the Foundation Trustees were important and powerful people, including Hollywood stars, corporate presidents, bankers, and politicians. Chief among these was Doctor George Piness, Loretta Young, Mr. and Mrs. Fritz Burns, and Mr. and Mrs. Harold McAlister, who spearheaded fundraising for the building program that resulted in the modernization and expansion of St. Anne's. The Foundation had a dues-paying membership of over 200 persons, and was led by a lay Board of Trustees which had about 30 members. The six auxiliaries of St. Anne's were part of the Foundation and included Sister Winifred Auxiliary, Josephine Brant Auxiliary, Loretta Young Auxiliary, Mabel Mosler Auxiliary, Helen Clark Auxiliary, and the Pilot Auxiliary. These adjuncts were semi-autonomous and all together had over 1,000 active members. We also had a very prestigious group, St. Anne's Guild, which was formed in 1938, and had a "Blue Book" membership of about 270 women in 1970. The Juniors of St. Anne's Guild was initially made up of the daughters of the Guild members, and there was a men's auxiliary too—The Joachim League. I spent most of my time in those days attending the functions of these many guilds and auxiliaries, which were providing a substantial part of the operating budget.

St. Anne's had a contract with the Los Angeles Department of Social Services (this was before there was a separate Department of Children and Family Services) and they paid St. Anne's a rate which, as I recall, was about $300 per month for girls living in St. Anne's residence. Girls did not need to be "placed" by the Department. We were paid for each girl we admitted, without any "red tape".

This led to a crisis in 1975 when Los Angeles County changed the procedure, and stopped paying for residents unless they were placed through the Departments of Social Services or Probation. Most of the residents at this time were self-placed or sent to St. Anne's by their parents, and we faced a substantial loss of revenue. At this time, Assemblyman Terry Goggin of San Bernardino was our friend in the State legislature. He was the nephew of longtime St. Anne's volunteer, Marguerite Lonergan, and was receptive to our request for a state law that would continue to pay for maternity home services. Since abortions were available to California residents at state expense, he devised a Bill that would also require the state to pay for maternity care for those who chose not to abort. The logic he argued was that the State should not incentivize abortions without offering an alternative. The Bill, AB 1069, called "The Pregnancy Freedom of Choice Act" passed the legislature and became effective in 1976. Thus, St. Anne's continued to offer services, with State reimbursement. Throughout the 1980's, this program was the primary revenue source. Only after the opening of the new residence in 1992 did we begin to focus our services on girls placed by the Departments of Children and Family Service or Probation.

Another crisis arose around the same time. The medical staff of St. Anne's Hospital had fewer and fewer doctors available to continue the services. As societal norms changed and medical care became more sophisticated, it was clear that the need for the anonymity of a maternity hospital was no longer necessary or prudent.

With major medical centers available and nearby, the decision was made to close St. Anne's Hospital in the autumn of 1976.

Thereafter, St. Anne's residents were taken to Queen of Angels Medical Center for delivery. Everything about St. Anne's was organized around the operation of the hospital, and it was a major revenue source. Closing it raised the question of whether St. Anne's could continue as a residence only. Approximately half of the employees were terminated, and there was a substantial reassignment of duties and responsibilities for those who remained. As I recall, 1977 was a lean and scary year, but we made it, and thereafter continued to thrive with the help of many volunteers and the gracious support of foundations and individual donors.

In 1987, the Board of Directors decided to again take on a major building program to improve St. Anne's facilities. At first, the prospect of a $13 million goal seemed overwhelming. But again, the leadership of Directors, Trustees and volunteers made it possible, and the Fritz and Gladys Burns building was opened in 1992. During the planning, we assumed St. Anne's would continue to serve girls only during their pregnancy, and it was designed with this intent. However, circumstances changed during the years we were building, and by the time it opened, we saw the need to provide a limited residence program for new mothers and their babies. This required some makeshift alterations to accommodate a nursery and child care center to care for babies while mothers were in school, and rooms designed for two teenaged girls became rooms for a mother and her baby.

While much has changed at St. Anne's in the past one hundred years, there remains a solid, values-based program of services for girls who are pregnant or parenting, with dedicated volunteers providing leadership, support and direction, and the continued prayerful sponsorship of the Franciscan Sisters of the Sacred Heart. The next hundred years should be easier!

The decade of the 1970's generated a new society in many ways and St. Anne's was positioned to meet the challenges as the profile of pregnant teens changed.

An article that appeared in the *Wall Street Journal*, April 23, 1974, noted that because birth rates in the East had dipped, a Cleveland hospital was retraining its OB nurses in other specialties and the maternity unit was converted into a psychiatric hospital. Chicago, Ohio and even a Los Angeles hospital reported similar birthrate declines.

St. Anne's received a call about the "closure" of their facility. That was news to the Sisters. The chronicles of the Franciscan Sisters indicated that St. Anne's was actually recruiting for nurses! The summer 1974 issue of the *Angel Messenger* reported that in the prenatal section of the hospital where the pregnant women resided, 520 women were cared for and an average daily census of 97.8% (a census meaning the count of women occupying the rooms). The average length of stay of was 62.5 days. The hospital admitted 663 and delivered 585 for a total of 589 live births. The Social Service Department fielded 1,483 inquiries, 908 intake appointments, and registered 896 total cases. McAlister High School even had 19 graduates in 1974. St. Anne's was far from closing![44]

St. Anne's excellent record can be compared to a 1975 article in the Ladies Home Journal that named a major Texas Hospital one of the 10 best hospitals for women in America, shaving an already reduced infant mortality rate from 40 deaths per 1,000 to 20 per 1,000. In 1974 and 1975, there were 1,064 births at St. Anne's with an infant mortality of four—which is five times better than the rate at the Texas hospital.

By the early 1970's, sixteen groups supported, directed and served St. Anne's Maternity Hospital: the Board of Directors, medical staff, Board of Trustees, St. Anne's Hospital Guild, Juniors of St. Anne's Hospital Guild, Orange County Guild of St. Anne's Hospital, Ventura County Guild of St. Anne's Hospital, Josephine Brant Auxiliary of St. Anne's Foundation, Helen Clark Auxiliary of St. Anne's Foundation,

Medical Staff – St. Anne's Maternity Hospital:
Seated left to right: Dr. Robert Kelly, Dr. Stephen Van adelsberg,
Dr. Venusteano Pulido, Dr. Chester Bonoff, Dr. Elmer Crehan
Standing left to right: Dr. Thomas O'Neill, Dr. Clyde Von der Ahe,
Dr. Jack Murrietta, Dr. John Thom

Mabel Mosler Auxiliary of St. Anne's Foundation, Loretta Young Auxiliary of St. Anne's Foundation, Sister Winifred Auxiliary of St. Anne's Foundation, Joachim League of St. Anne's Hospital, Las Anita's Auxiliary, Pilot Auxiliary of St. Anne's Hospital, and St. Anne's Coordinating Council.

St. Anne's may have been Los Angeles' best kept secret, however, many might have asked:

What is St. Anne's?[45]

An *Angel Messenger* (a publication of the hospital) described what St. Anne's was all about:

St. Anne's is:
❈ A place n the city of Los Angeles just a few short blocks from the Civic Center.

❧ A place that is much more than just a collection of bricks and stone and mortar.

❧ An attitude—a state of mind—a charitable institution.

❧ A place of love and care and a symbol of hope to the young unmarried girl who is pregnant out-of-wedlock and who wants to have her baby.

❧ A social casework agency with six full-time social workers, and a full-time psychologist and psychiatric consultants for the girls who turn to us for help, all located in the Sister Mary Winifred Clinic and Social Service Wing.

❧ A complete medical management of the unwed pregnancy with daily prenatal clinic and post-partum clinics, conducted by the same doctors in charge of delivery at the adjacent Queen of Angels Medical Center.

❧ A place offering classes in problems of labor, problems of pregnancy, nutrition during pregnancy, dental care, child care, parenting, budgeting, and all the other myriad of problems that face these young women.

❧ A 125-student junior and senior high school where girls continue their education. This building on the St. Anne's campus also houses vocational training programs, including market cashiering and operating a telephone switchboard, to help prepare the girl for a marketable skill after she delivers her baby.

❧ The Margaret Aicher dining room where balanced, nutritious meals are prepared and served daily to insure a normal, safe delivery and a healthy baby.

❧ A complete program of educational, recreational and spiritual activities designed to help each girl have a better realization of those areas which have not been a part of her life-style. The Msgr. Thomas J. O'Dwyer Chapel is open 24-hours-a-day for services and for prayer and meditation with a full-time chaplain at St. Anne's as well as the Franciscan Sisters of the Sacred Heart who staff St. Anne's.

❀ The foundation room where special theater parties are held for girls, rap sessions are conducted, dinners are given, and where the more than 1,000 volunteers meet their various groups to support St. Anne's.

❀ A group of caring people who provide guidance, counseling and love to the unmarried pregnant girl while helping to repair fractured family communication lines and helping her to determine the best plan for her and her baby.

❀ St. Anne's is love—and it is the carrying out of the teaching of Jesus when he told us to be our brother's keeper—"to do unto others as we would have others do unto us."

CARDINAL TIMOTHY MANNING
ARCHBISHOP 1970-1973
CARDINAL 1973-1985

In 1970, Coadjutor Archbishop Manning acceded to the See as the third Archbishop of Los Angeles. Three years later, he became the second cardinal for the largest city in the world dedicated to Our Blessed Mother. For fifteen years, the Irish born prelate prevailed through enormous changes in the Church aided by four auxiliary bishops for the three-county area (Los Angeles, Ventura, and Santa Barbara) for in 1976 Orange County was separated into the Diocese of Orange. Cardinal Manning ordained the first permanent deacon class for the archdiocese in 1975 and by the end of his episcopate, the Catholic population was close to two and a half million. As bishop, he confirmed over 650,000 young people. He died in 1989.

The chronicles of the Franciscan Sisters on January 7, 1977 stated that St. Anne's filed a notice with the County Clerk to do business as St. Anne's Maternity Home although the legal title remained St. Anne's Maternity Hospital, a non-profit corporation of the State of California. Since at least 1938, St. Anne's has been in her title.

Nationally, the unwed pregnancies continued to rise. In 1940, there were 39.9 (4%) unwed pregnancies per 1,000 live births; in 1976, it was 147.8 and by 1977, there were 238 (24%). In less than 40 years, the rate had increased six times over. A study conducted by St. Anne's revealed that single parents age 15-19 in 1966 had 12,819 births, which increased steadily until it decreased slightly in 1971; in 1972, the increase started again, growing steadily in 1977; the last year figures were available totaling 24,225 births.[46]

The California live birth rate continued to rise in the 1970's, as well as for unmarried women, ages 15-19: 20.6 per 1,000 in 1971 to 27.3 per 1,000 in 1977. In Los Angeles County 28,256 out of 118,705 live births were to single parents.[47]

St. Anne's persistently met the needs of unwed pregnant mothers but as society changed in the 1970's, the prohibitive expense of malpractice insurance and other operating costs, made it necessary to limit the facilities at St. Anne's. In September 1976, St. Anne's closed its hospital wing and transferred delivery and post-partum services to their own private section at Queen of Angels Hospital.

The closure of the hospital services wing brought a significant change for St. Anne's. The challenged institution sought ways to use the vacant space. As these were explored, the closed areas were even used for filming Hollywood movies. One concept discussed included renting the space for offices to non-profit organizations.

Another idea was to convert it to a long-term care facility, which would have involved mixing St. Anne's teenage girls with elderly ladies residing in assisted living or skilled nursing unit. At one point we considered an intergenerational program under the auspices of the

Sister Dismas Janssen, Sister Agnes Kulas and Sister Marina Scholl – Circa 1970's

Sr. M. Clare Van Vooren, Sr. M. Gerard Lopez, Sr. M. Pauline Racich, Sr. Mariella Miller, Sr. Luitgardis Totzki – Circa 1979

Fr. Herbert and Residents – Circa 1980's

Sister Anthony Clare Floto

Patio

Pool for Residents' Use – Circa 1970

Ethel Percie Andres Center at USC, a younger population of pregnant girls with an older population of women working together to help each other.

Occasionally, legislative milestones affect choices. In 1977, legislation known as AB 1069 Freedom of Choice Act, was signed by Governor Edward G. Brown, and became effective on January 1, 1978. This gave unwed pregnant teenagers an alternative to abortion, providing complete equity with abortion laws for teen-age California girls who are pregnant out-of-wedlock and want to carry their babies to term.

Essentially, AB1069 provided that any unmarried pregnant girls under the age of 21 could request and receive maternity home services either at their request or that of their parents without being asked for financial support. The bill also assured that such care could not be denied by any governmental agency. The care was partially paid through a newly-created state program. Up until this time, girls who asked for an abortion could receive it without parental consent, but the girls who elected to carry their babies to term could receive very little financial assistance, and frequently they could not obtain maternity home services without their parents' consent.[48]

Assemblyman Terry Goggin introduced earlier legislation but it expired on December 31, 1977. Mr. Goggin was a strong supporter of St. Anne's and her mission.

From 1908 to the late 1970's, the girl who came to St. Anne's came to hide. The scenario was typically a middle-class white girl of 17 or 18 who got pregnant; whose baby was given up for adoption and then the girl quietly dropped back into society. She often had a subconscious need to be pregnant, a desire to be a mother. One of the reasons may have been to find someone to love and love her back. Sixty-five percent of the girls planned to keep their babies and raise them as single parents, compared with a state and national average of 94%.

St. Anne's was serving between 800 and 1,000 unwed pregnant girls each year. To support the mission, there was a core of 21 doctors and dentists, 1,200 lay volunteers and 40 employees. St. Anne's conducted studies to determine the means of meeting the needs of unwed mothers who keeps their babies. In 1975, 14% of live births in Southern California were out-of-wedlock while 80,000 abortions were performed in Los Angeles. As it had done for decades, St. Anne's was prepared to confront the challenges with confidence and "quiet assurance."[49]

Sister Margaret Anne Floto, part of the leadership team of the Franciscan Sisters, was appointed chairman of the board in 1980, a position she held with distinction for the next 17 years.

The Weingart Foundation donated a two-story apartment building in 1982, located on the corner of Beverly Boulevard and Reno Street. St. Anne's was able to develop a half-way house for girls who planned to live independently but were not

Sister Margaret Anne Floto

quite prepared to go out on their own. This arrangement assisted them until they were able to live without the assistance St. Anne's provided.

GATEWAY HOUSE
Located in Pomona, this small facility offered apartments for five mothers and their babies, counseling, assistance in caring for their children, aid and encouragement to finish school and find meaningful employment or job training. (See Notes, pages 126-127)

Gateway House, in Pomona, offered apartments for five young single mothers to live with their babies during the transition to independent living.

QUEENSCARE FAMILY CLINICS

During 1982, Queen of Angels Clinic moved to St. Anne's Clinic wing and began to provide prenatal care for residents as well as medical care to the general community. By 2008, QueensCare Family Clinics was still providing services on the campus. (See Notes, page 129)

OUTREACH

Adapting to the needs in the community, St. Anne's began a new program in 1987, to assist girls who did not need extensive services associated with residential care. This was accomplished in group sessions, crisis counseling and referral, prenatal and child care education, including follow-up with former residents, and pregnancy prevention education. The social workers operated in Los Angeles County in a cooperative effort with five established facilities: Gateway House in Pomona, three Thread of Life homes—Mar Vista, Norwalk, and San Fernando; in Central Los Angeles at St. Anne's, and later at La Cuna Pregnancy Clinic in South Central Los Angeles, Ventura and Santa Barbara Counties. Transition group sessions were offered each week at McAlister High School on campus. Outreach provided the education for the girls, focusing on vocational and educational opportunities and referrals on other services available in the community. Over 600 additional girls took part annually in the outreach services. (See Notes, pages 134-136)

Values clarification that centered on moral, ethical and religious ideals were part of the responsible teen sexuality education. This gave the adolescents an opportunity to discuss personal goals and to understand how premature sexual activity can negatively affect those goals by diminishing their future hopes and dreams.[50] By 2006, the outreach services essentially were subsumed into the Family Based Services.

VILLA MAJELLA

In 1982 an independent group of people united in the belief that Santa Barbara needed to do more for pregnant, unwed young women, bought a four-bedroom house and named it Villa Majella. The word 'Majella' is taken from St. Gerard Majella, patron saint of expectant mothers. Its purpose was to shelter pregnant young women who otherwise would have nowhere to go. The Villa Majella Board of Directors ran the home for five years, developing a program over time. Mary Klink, one of the founding members, said "If you're going to tell women that abortion is wrong, then you need to provide an alternative…my belief in the sanctity of life compelled me to action."[51] From this conviction, Villa Majella was founded. St. Anne's assumed sponsorship from 1987 to 1995 when the Villa Majella Board of Directors reassumed the responsibility of the home. (See Notes, pages 129-130)

Villa Majella – Santa Barbara

FACILITIES PLANNING

The leadership of St. Anne's in 1982 engaged planner Lou Gelwicks and his firm, Gerontological Planning Associates. The Gelwicks organization conducted a number of studies in the early 1980's on the quality of facilities on the campus and ways they could be adapted for the elderly. These efforts included marketing and feasibility studies.

Conceptually, a gradual evolution took place to convert the bricks and mortar, i.e., part of the facility, into services for the elderly, a growing population in need of assisted living and nursing care. Theoretically, St. Anne's could make this a profitable operation and use the revenue to fund community-based services for pregnant and parenting teens.

St. Anne's also explored models of effective service for pregnant teenagers. This was conducted by Elsa Pauley from UCLA. Her study revealed that it was equally effective and more feasible to provide counseling and outreach programs to pregnant and parenting teens than by offering institutional services. St. Anne's had a reputation, not only for care of pregnant teens but also as a supplier of residential care.

In the early 1980's, St. Anne's adopted a mission statement to include long term care of the elderly. By 1986, it was clear that part of the facilities built in the 1940's and the old cottages, constructed at the turn of the century located next to St. Anne's, needed to be replaced.

St. Anne's engaged another planning firm, Stone Marraccini & Patterson and the architectural firm of Haynes & Oakley, who worked with St. Anne's management and Board to create a new facilities master plan in September 1987. The plan's three phases called for: 1) gradual acquisition of property on the south side of Glassell Street not owned by St. Anne's. Eventually, it would lead to closing Glassell Street to create one and a half blocks (an enclosed campus); 2) construction of a new residential maternity home where the old single story frame structures once stood; 3) build an assisted living facility that would be connected to the maternity home structure. This master plan guided the development of St. Anne's campus over the ensuing 20 years, except that instead of developing an assisted living facility for seniors, St. Anne's Board, with approval of the Franciscan Sisters, decided instead to construct transitional living apartments and an early learning center. The Capital Campaign began in 1988-89 to raise about $13 million for this 1992 structure, and foundations were approached for grants.

During 1988, the Board of Directors began to consider a major shift in the program, to provide housing, not just for pregnant teenagers, but also teen mothers and their infants who have no other place to live. St. Anne's redefined its scope to address the broader issue of teen pregnancy as a whole. This redefinition placed St. Anne's more accurately in the social milieu of the time, offering a Christian response to the problem of teen pregnancy. The questions posed dealt with teenage sexual behavior, parenting or adoption, and financial responsibility: What was the root cause of teen pregnancy? And how were moral values formed? These and other concerns were dealt with directly and it was through the curriculum of junior and senior high schools to encourage responsibility toward teenage sexuality. Teen pregnancy was and *is* part of a complex set of problems including poverty, physical, sexual and substance abuse.[52]

In the decades since it was founded, St. Anne's transformed victimized young women into caring and capable parents, students, employees, and community members. From 1992-2007, St. Anne's experienced some of the most striking programs and service changes in its history. The traditional maternity home as it was known ceased to exist.

RESIDENTIAL EDUCATION AND TREATMENT

In the 1990's, St. Anne's was licensed for 60 residents and 42 babies and it still operated as a traditional maternity home. An enhanced residential education program offered the young women classes in prenatal health care, prepared childbirth/Lamaze, postpartum health care, child development, parenting, adolescent sexuality education, life skills, tutoring, and personal development. Interns from area schools and educational centers also came to St. Anne's which presented an excellent training ground to expand the education of the interns. Clinical services were provided by licensed social workers who served as liaisons with the residents and outside agencies. (See Notes, pages 131-134)

St. Anne's broke ground in 1991 for a $13.3 million building project. The courts were dealing with an increased number of abused and neglected adolescent girls. And as the construction progressed, fewer girls were entering St. Anne's on a voluntary basis and more calls were received

*Bishop John J. Ward,
City Councilman John Ferraro,
Foundation Board Chair Evelyn Blasiar
at groundbreaking for new residence*

*Sister Margaret Anne
and Sister Marina
join friends at the
1991 groundbreaking*

*St. Anne, Grandmother of Jesus,
with her daughter, St. Mary*

*Franciscan Sisters of the Sacred Heart, Frankfort, Illinois,
gather for a community celebration, 2004*

**Christ and the Children of the "World"
A Mural by Isabel Piczek**

*Located in St. Anne's chapel, the mural
takes reference from Luke 18:16–17
and John 15:5. In this world of cold
sophistication and disbelief, Christ puts
the image of the child in front of our
eyes, which is an image of simplicity,
belief, and above all, love. Hence the
expressions of the children's faces on
the mural. This work of art is
representative of the mission at
St. Anne's of caring for pregnant
adolescents, young mothers, and their
babies of all creeds, races and cultures.*

Artist rendering of St. Anne's expansion – 1992

Foundation Room – Conference Center

Front entrance lobby with balcony walkway

Gladys & Fritz B. Burns Residence – 1992

Side of chapel, front entrance and
residence towers

Side entrance on Occidental
Street, showing the Column
Residence Living Towers

The patio
coming from the
Foundation
Room

Residence – 1992: A typical bedroom for a girl

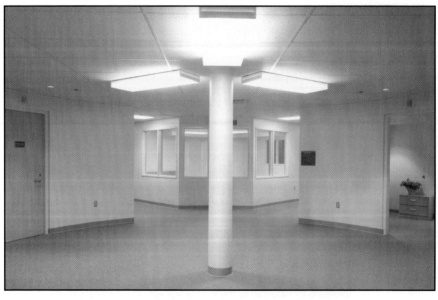

Each column living quarters has a living room (room in background).

Bogen Family Center: Transitional Housing and Early Learning Center – 2005

New Villiage Charter High School – 2006
In renovated McAlister High School building

*Happy children at the
Bogen Family Center*

from the County of Los Angeles for placement. Once again a different focus was needed. Before 1992, the girls did not come back to St. Anne's after the delivery of their babies. But if the girls were to return with their babies after delivery, as the need suggested, further modification of the girls' rooms and services was necessary.

The new Gladys and Fritz Burns Residence was completed and the facility was blessed on February 13, 1992 officiated by the Most Reverend John J. Ward, Auxiliary Bishop of Los Angeles Archdiocese, Our Lady of the Angels Pastoral Region. (See Notes, page 130-131)

The new wing included a small mother-baby unit, initially for six beds. But the mothers also needed a place where they and their babies could receive care while the mothers finished school. That program was in high demand and by 2002, there were 24 beds.

Mr. and Mrs. Fritz Burns

About 1994-95, an all-day board planning retreat considered their mission statement that called for care of the elderly as part of the mission. Differing views revealed concerns about moving away from our traditional focus while others saw it as an appropriate expansion and a valid use of the facilities. The board decided to eliminate care of the elderly as part of the mission which led to the idea of an apartment building, not for the elderly, but for parenting teenagers emancipating from the foster care system.

The master facilities plan designated that St. Anne's control acquiring all the property adjacent to the facility and this took several years, which culminated in 1997. St Anne's petitioned the City of Los Angeles to close Glassell Street, since all of the property on both sides was owned by St. Anne's.

The Burns wing included a Foundation Room and Conference Center that was made available to the community for seminars, workshops, training sessions, conferences, meetings and banquets. This was a source of additional revenue for the group home which helped to defray some of the facility's operating costs. This has been a very popular and useful service.

St. Anne's six-acre campus in central Los Angeles was also home to other agencies that offered assistance to children in need and other disadvantaged persons, including Aviva Center, Child & Family Services Day Care Center, Child Welfare League of America, Children's Bureau/NuParent, LAUSD's McAlister High School for pregnant and parenting students, Southern California Foster Family & Adoption Agency. The rental income helped St. Anne's provide its services.

MOTHER/BABY PROGRAM

Prior to 1992, the girls did not stay in residence after the birth of their babies. All this changed with the introduction of residential care for adolescent mothers with children in the new Mother/Baby Program.

For over 80 years, St. Anne's cared for pregnant teens, but the need to expand services to include mothers and their babies required St. Anne's to refocus the care being provided. The new unit was designed to house 96 teenagers. The required shift in programs and services to two populations changed the environment of St. Anne's. The girls' stay in the prenatal unit was short term, about 3 or 4 months. St. Anne's was now looking at longer term for residents with babies and the designated space for mother and babies grew. Prenatal clients were housed on the third floor where two teens shared a room. In the mother/baby program, the infant/child was housed in the same room with the mother.

TRIUMPH OVER ADVERSITY

By Afrodita Fuentes

Duglugolecki

Afrodita Fuentes with son Robert

In July 1991, I was just 14 years old when I ran away from my home in Guatemala with my boyfriend. We arrived in the City of Angels on September 6, 1991. I felt, at this vulnerable age, extremely lonely, living in a foreign place where I didn't speak any English and didn't know anyone. I felt lost and struggled to assimilate it all.

My boyfriend, Carlos, was a much older man and less than two months in Los Angeles, I found myself pregnant. After a few months of just staying in the apartment with morning sickness, Carlos and I decided that I would go to school.

When I gave my personal information to the school, the school personnel got concerned about my pregnancy and my relationship with an older man. They called the authorities. The police came to the school and brought me to St. Anne's. A few days later, I went back to Carlos because everything was so unfamiliar to me and I wanted to be with him. The Department of Children and Family Services searched for me and I was sent to McLaren Hall, a group home in El Monte, California. This place was scary. It was very crowded and there were all kinds of children with very serious problems.

January 1992 was one of the saddest and most frightening months of my life—I cried day and night! According to the staff, I was well-behaved and so I earned "points" to buy a grey teddy bear that gave me some comfort. I did meet a "normal girl" named Maria and she listened to my cries for a few days, but then her parents came for her. I really did not want to be there, so I begged to be brought back to St. Anne's because I knew that it was the only place that could give me the stability, safety and tranquility I so desperately needed for myself and my baby.

In February of 1992, I was already four months pregnant when I returned to St. Anne's. Having felt so isolated and alone before this, I found the protected, caring environment there a welcome change. I no longer worried about shelter, food or safety. I immersed myself in school learning, English and doing something productive. I just did not want to think that I did not have family and close friends in this country and that soon I had to take care of myself and a baby.

From the time I got to Los Angeles, I wrote monthly letters home to my family in Guatemala. My main purpose was to let my mother know I was OK because she had been worried sick since I left. My father was immensely angry that I had disgraced the family. It is still painful to think about my father's constant anger and intimidation when I was growing up, and even reading it in some of the letters he sent me. Ultimately, what determined my stay in the U.S. was a telephone call with my parents monitored by the Department of Children and Family services, where my father spoke to me in his usual frightening manner. Now, in a way, my father recognizes that he was too harsh with his children.

When it neared time for me to deliver my baby, I was afraid I would have to leave St. Anne's soon afterwards. I was scared that once again I would find myself with nowhere to go, this time with a very young child. Luckily, just two days before my son Robert was born, St. Anne's created a new program that would allow me to continue living there after delivery and help me to learn to take care of myself and a newborn baby. Robert was the first baby born into St. Anne's new Mother & Baby Program, a precursor to today's Residential Treatment Program. I made friendships with St. Anne's staff members that would influence me for years to come, many with whom I remain in close contact.

Carlos and I exchanged letters for about a year. He was able to meet our son when Robert was 15-months old. Our problems continued and a few months later, the relationship came to a complete stop.

While learning how to care for my new child, I continued excelling at school. With a private tutor, I learned to speak, read and write English. I transferred to Belmont High School and focused on what I needed to do to graduate and get into college. St. Anne's helped me become involved with the Big Sisters of Los Angeles, where I was paired with a Big Sister, Sara Tyndal. I also took advantage of opportunities to volunteer at a local hospital, worked part-time in St. Anne's Development Department, and began selling AVON products to earn extra money. I focused on my future!

My counselor at this time was Steve Gunther, who now serves as St. Anne's Chief Operating Officer. Steve listened to me and helped me so much. He co-signed the AVON contract and even drove me to my college interview. He was a wonderful advocate.

I was accepted at Mt. St. Mary's College. The summer before I started school, Robert and I left St. Anne's and rented a room from my Big Sister, Sara. In May of 2001, I graduated with a BS in Biology. Since then, I've taught Biology at Belmont High School, where I was once a student. I also earned my secondary teaching credential.

In 2007, I worked toward on my Masters in Science Education at California State University, Northridge. Graduation is anticipated in May of 2008. After that plans are to continue with my goals to teach abroad and achieve my National Board Certification in teaching. Robert looks forward to accompanying me when it's time to go overseas and would love going to school in a foreign country. At one point in my teaching career I would like to do scientific research with my students in collaboration with universities and organizations around the world. I also hope to own a house some day!

Voluntary placements were the tradition until 1992; a girl entered the facility of her own free will. With the advent of the Mother/Baby Program, pregnant and parenting adolescents were placed either by the Department of Children and Family Services or the Probation Department. All were under State protection and had been removed from their home due to abuse or neglect. They suffered from a many problems that complicated their lives, had been sexually and/or physically abused (79% of the residents) or had been abandoned in their early childhoods.

Around 1992, studies showed that 65% of adolescents who became parents have, themselves been victims of abuse. These girls have suffered such abuse as highlighted in these examples:[53]

* ❉ A 13-year old sold by her parents to a 24-year old man; she became pregnant, the man kicked her out; she returned to her family and was told she was an embarrassment and no longer a part of the family.
* ❉ A 15-year old who was beaten so ruthlessly by the father of her baby that she was brought under state protection.
* ❉ Another 15-year old who has not seen her mother sober once in the past six years.

❅ A tragic story of a 15-year old whose parents had offered the state custody because they "don't want her any more."

❅ A 17-year old whose mother fled to Florida without telling her. She later sent her daughter a note saying she was no longer interested in being a mother.

The interventions and services at St Anne's strive to break the cycle of abuse to prevent these teens from becoming abusers themselves.

FROM ABUSE TO WHOLENESS

By Machelle Massey

Before coming to St. Anne's, I lived with my alcoholic mother, who had three children by the time she was 18, one the result of my grandfather molesting her. My mother came from a long life of abuse and became an abuser herself. When I was only four years old, I would be left alone for days with my brother. When I wasn't being neglected, I was physically and mentally abused; my mother beat me with anything she could grab: shoes, curling irons, spoons, belts, brushes, a clothes iron, whatever was handy.

Machelle Massey with daughter Jazzmen

When I first came to St. Anne's, I was violent and angry. I had no remorse for anything I did. I was very hard, very stubborn, basically a brick wall. I wanted to hurt anyone and everyone, even if they weren't the people who had hurt me.

While at St. Anne's, I took anger management classes. I really needed those classes. My social worker was wonderful; she waited for me to open up to her. I sat in her office silent for a whole year and she worked with me so patiently. She eventually got me to open up and work on my anger and other issues.

I attribute my good parenting skills to my time at St. Anne's. I'm there for my daughter, whatever she needs—her performances, and her homework. I take her to school and pick her up. I'm very involved. My daughter attends a performing arts school, and she's a great student. Because of St. Anne's, I feel like good things have happened to me, but I look at my little girl and think great things can happen for her.

I now work as an Educational Community Worker for the L.A. County Office of Education/Foster Youth Services. I've come full circle helping teens in the foster care system get an education. I was married in November of 2006 and I am now living a happy full life with my daughter, Jazzmen, and husband, Damon.

CHILD DEVELOPMENT CENTER (CDC)

In addition to housing the mothers with children, St. Anne's needed a place for child care in the residential unit which needed to be retro-fitted. The challenge of the CDC was to create healthy childhoods for their children where mothers learned to be good parents even though they hadn't received good parenting themselves. This creative program to educate mothers in parenting translated baby care into reality. (See Notes, pages 131-134)

St. Anne's educational achievements were recognized in Los Angeles County: The Enrichment Plus Program award of Merit for Best Educational Alliance from the County of Los Angeles/ Department of Children and Family Services. It acknowledges outstanding achievements in academic performance, partnerships with teachers, and future opportunities for children, and commitment to academic excellence. The award given in 1999 cited St. Anne's outstanding collaboration with LAUSD, the Los Angeles Educational Partnership, the Community College Foundation, and the Department of Children and Family Services. The award is evidence of the standard of excellence in the facility's academic programs.[54]

In 2001, St. Anne's was honored for its efforts on behalf of residents' education by the Los Angeles County Department of Children and Family Services' "Finest Education Alliance Award."[55]

In 1996, Governor Pete Wilson identified the unwed pregnant teenager one of the highest priorities of state government. "A social problem considered so dangerous that it threatens every facet of life in California, from schools and police departments to the resources available for environmental and transportation departments." The Governor marshaled its resources to address the issue, "This is the most basic, fundamental social problem of our day." Bill Lockyear, California State Legislator, emphasized the same idea, "We have to change that behavior."

At the time, the state spent up to $7 billion each year just on welfare to families produced by teenage mothers. Governor Wilson warned that, "70,000 births to California teens each year create an enormous burden for a variety of public safety, education and social service systems as well as a perceptible degradation in the state's quality of life. The consequences for them, and for us, are devastating, but when we succeed, we can build fewer prisons and more college libraries."[56]

St. Anne's has always been about nurturing in an environment of love, care and concern. It is all about healing, learning, individual and family growth, and personal responsibility. "Every birth is a miracle, no matter how inopportune the timing. It is our goal at St. Anne's to prepare our girls in the very best way possible for the birth of their babies. We nurture them so they can nurture their babies. In this way, we shelter the birth of the new life that comes to us."[57]

Comparative statistics illustrate best the success of St. Anne's programs:[58]

	California Teen Mothers	St. Anne's Residents
Receiving welfare 18 months after birth of child	72%	24%
Graduation from high school	20%	85%
Additional pregnancies	22%	12%
Low birth weight (under 5.8 lbs.)	11%	5%
Baby relinquished for adoption	5%	22%

Andy Bogen of Gibson, Dunn & Crutcher was appointed chairman of the board in 1999. "As I see it, St. Anne's mission is to provide an opportunity for a rewarding and productive life to young women and their infants who are at a serious risk of missing out on that life. It is a private, safe, and secure atmosphere for young women facing the challenge of pregnancy and mothering under difficult circumstances."[59]

In the 2000's, 33% of teens who begin families before the age of 18 never complete high school. But statistics of St. Anne's residents show a high percent of the girls achieve high school graduation or complete GED requirements. While there were many more in residents, out of 20 girls of graduation age, 15 (75%) graduated, despite the many risk factors these young women brought with them to St. Anne's. Every day hundreds of children pass through the seemingly endless cycle of California's child welfare system. Many bounce from foster home to foster home, never knowing the support and love of a secure family environment. In 1994, more than 91,000 children were part of California's foster care system—which comes to about one-fifth of all children in foster care nationwide.[60] The shelter and services that St. Anne's offers are now an integral part of California's child welfare system.

Creating Your Future[61]
By Jillian Howden

Creating your future, it's about your dreams
You have the ability, you have the means.
To create whatever you want, you choose,
When you see your future, you can't lose.
Because it's all about your goals and dreams,
When times are down it sometimes seems,
Like your future isn't so bright,
But all you need is to know what's right.
For you and only you, to yourself you must be true
As you choose your future means to be dedicated,
Strong to pursue those dreams.

In 2001, nearly half of the children in the foster care system of Los Angeles County became homeless a year after leaving the system. This alarming statistic moved the Governing Board of St. Anne's to action. With an initial gift from the Fritz Burns Foundation, St. Anne's began formulating a plan and in 2002 assembled a team of professionals including ONYX Architects and Walton Construction Company to begin the design of a housing complex. In 2003, an ambitious capital campaign began.

In the meantime, after serving two terms as interim leader of St. Anne's, Tony Walker, MA was appointed President and CEO in 2003, following the 30-year leadership of Tom Owenson. "Our mandate is to provide the young women we serve with the tools necessary to achieve in the future."[62] Tony Walker had 31 years of experience as a senior manager and consultant in the field of child welfare and mental health.

He arrived at the time of the capital campaign, "Building Futures" which set a $13 million goal. Groundbreaking took place on February 23, 2004 and in 15 months the campaign successfully raised the necessary funds from public and private resources.

Tony Walker, MA
St. Anne's President/CEO

MENTAL HEALTH SERVICES

In 2003, St. Anne's contracted with the County of Los Angeles for mental health services, expanding far beyond the initial clinical services provided in the residential program. This helped to provide essential funding for the total treatment program at St. Anne's. The resident who came into St. Anne's had experienced much turmoil especially due to multiple out-of-home placements. More than 87% of St. Anne's residents have been in out-of-home placements and about half of them, four or more placements. These teens were removed from the home because of substance abuse and/or neglect.

The emotional and psychological needs of the residents were more intense, requiring a more comprehensive approach. The mental health services give the residents' psychotherapy, counseling, and group therapy that targets substance abuse, domestic violence, and anger management. With the Los Angeles County Department of Mental Health, St. Anne's helps address severe emotional and behavioral disorders inflicting those with which more than 90% of the residents struggle. The teens suffered from depression (89%), impulsive disorder (44%), suicidal ideation (34%) and chemical abuse (44%).[63] This collaborative effort supports individual and family therapy, art and recreational therapy, and specialty groups that deal with the issues of substance abuse, teen relationships, domestic violence and victims of abuse.

THE BOGEN FAMILY CENTER

Named for board chair, Andrew Bogen and his wife, Deborah, Bogen Family Center was completed on schedule and under budget and was dedicated on June 23, 2005, officiated by Cardinal Roger Mahony, Archbishop of Los Angeles. There, components of the Bogen center included transitional housing and a children's center.

Transitional Housing

This was St. Anne's response to the serious lack of affordable housing for those emancipating from the foster care system. When it was built with a capacity for 39 young women, it was the largest of its kind in Los Angeles County serving this target population. The program offered two years of transitional housing and the necessary resources and support. This type of housing became a model for Los Angeles. These included childcare, mental health services, parent training, and the identification of resources that encouraged residents to become self-sufficient and contributing members of society.[64] By July 18th the first family moved into a Transitional Housing apartment. On the same day, the Early Learning Center began its service.

In its second year, the Bogen Family Center supplied affordable transitional housing services to 82 children and 68 young women, ages 18-24 that left foster care. Family advocates provided resources to help them obtain permanent housing, find meaningful employment, live independently, and parent effectively. The women and their child live in fully furnished one-bedroom apartments and are obliged to abide by certain rules during their residence at the center.

The supportive services included job training and development, education, self-empowerment workshops, medical and mental health care, parenting and child-care classes. The mothers are required to be in school and work up to 40 hours a week as well as attend on-site classes and counseling sessions.[65]

The Early Learning Center

The Early Learning Center more than tripled the capacity of the former CDC. It provided services for 126 children of the women from the residential treatment program, transitional housing and families in the surrounding community. The children were six weeks to five years of age.

The expert staff in the licensed Early Learning Center cared for 293 children. In the summer of 2006, there were 14 preschooler graduates and in 2007, 38 preschoolers graduated. St. Anne's expanded its full day of free quality childcare to 56 preschoolers, children of low-income families in the community. The success of the center comes in part from the successful partnerships established with Para Los Ninos, Kedren Community Health Center, and the Department of Children and Family Services. By 2007, 32 young women and 39 children successfully moved out of transitional housing into independent living.[66]

Mental Health Department

The Mental Health Department opened its doors to the community in 2004 and then launched the newly created Family Based Services Department in October 2005. The services included four programs solely dedicated to serving at-risk children and families living in the community: Family Literacy, Family Preservation, Wrap Around Approach Services and Partnership for Families Initiative.[67]

Before 2003, St. Anne's had operated only the residential treatment program. In less than three years, with the Los Angeles County

Mental Health partnership, St. Anne's expanded from one program to five: Mental Health, Early Learning Center, Residential Program, Family Based Services and Transitional Housing. From a little known haven offering shelter to pregnant teens in 1908, St. Anne's has developed a set of programs outside the walls of the facility, an anchor of service to the community as it was known in 2007.

CARDINAL ROGER M. MAHONY
ARCHBISHOP 1985-
CARDINAL 1991-

With Cardinal Manning's retirement in 1985, the archdiocese looked to Rome and Pope John Paul II for a successor. The pope named the first native born Angeleno for the largest archdiocese in the country—Bishop Roger Mahony who headed the Diocese of Stockton and was an alumnus of St. John's Seminary. In 1991, he became the third cardinal for the archdiocese that extends from Santa Maria to Orange County. He created the five Pastoral Regions for the archdiocese in 1986. In 1995, Cardinal Mahony announced plans to build the Cathedral of Our Lady of the Angels to replace St. Vibiana's. Dedication of the new Cathedral on temple Street was September 2, 2002.

The Archdiocese of Los Angeles comprises three counties – Los Angeles, Ventura and Santa Barbara – and covers 8,762 square miles. The total population is 11,012,763 with Catholic population of 4,448,763 as of January 2006. The 287 parishes are located in 120 cities in the five Pastoral Regions. The Diocese was established in 1840 and created an Archbishopric in 1936. The Patrons of the Archdiocese are Our Lady of the Angels, St. Vibiana, St. Patrick and St. Emydius.

JOURNEY TO SUCCESS

By Yecica Robles

Duglugolecki

Yecica Robles with son Carlos

I was only 14 years old when I came from Mexico to Los Angeles in 1999. My son, Carlos, and I, left my grandparent's home to live with my mother and step father. Carlos was just 11 months old. Prior to this move, I had seen my mother only a few times. I struggled to adapt to this new, strange environment, one which, as it turned out, wasn't necessarily the best for me or my son. I was in a foreign country, didn't speak any English, and was essentially living with strangers.

Less than two years later, Carlos and I were removed from my mother and stepfather's house and placed in a foster home. Over the next several years, I was moved several times, to other foster homes and finally ended up at Booth Memorial, a group home similar to St. Anne's that has since been closed. Throughout this, I suffered the consequences of not having stability; my high school graduation was delayed because I had not been enrolled in school for my first year in the U.S.; during my foster care placements I switched schools several times but also worked hard to learn English. Throughout this time I would say that the biggest challenge during the whole experience was trying to create a sense of safety for my son in these crazy environments.

But staying focused and working hard was never a problem for me. I knew that school was my ticket to a better future. On June 23, 2005, at the age of 20, just five years after I came to the U.S., I celebrated earning my high school diploma. Graduating and receiving my diploma on stage was one of my biggest dreams.

Coincidentally, June 23rd was the same day St. Anne's Bogen Family Center celebrated its grand opening. I had heard about the new housing since I had been living at another group home, when the facility was just beginning to be constructed. I told my social worker about it, and went to the orientation and was accepted. Carlos and I were among the first to move in to the center in August 2005.

While participating in the Transitional Housing Program, I became a Resident Manager, and worked with the on-site Property Manager. When that position became open, it seemed like a natural transition, and I eagerly took the job. As Property Manager I am responsible for handling all the paperwork required for new residents, managing daily facilities needs, and acting as an overall liaison with the program staff and residents.

In 2007, Carlos was eight years old and attending a local elementary school. I work as St. Anne's Transitional Housing Program's Property Manager and go to school at Los Angeles City College, taking a full course load. I am working hard to simultaneously earn my Real Estate License, taking classes to become a Certified Public Accountant, and taking general education classes, with the overall goal to earn a degree in Psychology and work as a mentor helping kids in foster care. I also find time to volunteer in community groups such as The Rampart Village Neighborhood Council, and I plan on volunteering during the summer break helping out at Rampart Police Station.

In 2007, I completed the Transitional Housing Program and continue to live on-site. This program has really opened a lot of doors for me. I feel really blessed to have such positive people on my side. I share my experience with the other residents and say, "The doors are there, you just need to want to open them. I think everything happens for a reason. I wouldn't be where I am today without going through what I have, and you just have to believe and work hard. If you do that, and follow the rules, you will be fine."

FAMILY BASED SERVICES (FBS)[68]

The child welfare field noted a growing trend: children fared better in home placements compared to residential care facilities, and when issues are addressed effectively, long-term disruption of the family unit can be avoided and/or reunification is resolved more quickly. St. Anne's Board of Directors and senior management team decided to provide children and families living "outside the walls" of St. Anne's with access to the comprehensive array of services and supports they needed most.

The four family-centered programs, designed to provide current and added support to families living at St. Anne's and in the local community, are consistent with our mission and vision statements.

Wrap-Around Approach: FBS uses a *"whatever it takes"* wrap-around approach with all families that receive services. Regardless of what specific program a family enrolls in, they can expect an individualized and strength-based assessment and service plan, community-based low or no-cost referrals and resources, in-home counseling and parenting support, 24-hour crisis response, and intensive case management. Some of the additional services participants may receive include, but are not limited to:

❀ Intensive services for special family needs with domestic violence; mental health; substance abuse.

❀ Family supports and access to safe, affordable, high quality early care and education.

❀ Referrals/Linkages: Job training & employment services; educational assistance; safe and affordable housing; Regional Center services.

Family Literacy: First Five LA (an organization that grew out of the California tobacco settlement) partners with St. Anne's to provide education and activities that promote early learning, health and safety to families with children, prenatal through age five. The program is dedicated to breaking the cycle of low educational achievement and poverty through learning and education. Participants are provided tools, resources and support as well cultural activities and field trips. All create and encourage meaningful learning opportunities for the entire family, emphasizing the role of parents in their child's overall development.

Family preservation: Through a partnership with Para Los Ninos, this integrated collaboration extends intensive services to at-risk children, preventing removal from the home when possible; it supports and encourages family reunification when appropriate. The profiles of these young people are similar to those in St. Anne's residential population. They are frequently victims of abuse and neglect, and risk long-term consequences, including repeating these cycles with their own children. St. Anne's provides the entire family unit with in-home outreach counseling as well as linking them to other agencies that can provide other services for their unique needs.

Partnership for Families: This initiative is funded by a partnership with Para Los Ninos, a multi-agency collaboration to bridge the gaps in the current child welfare system by developing and providing voluntary prevention services to at-risk pregnant and or parenting women. The families receive six months of counseling, housing assistance, child care, educational and vocational referrals, and parenting supports. The program offers challenged parents with young children tools and resources necessary to provide safe and loving homes for their children and to prevent abuse or maltreatment. Anyone residing in the residential programs is encouraged to participate.

In 2006, California was home to one out of five of the nation's foster children—the highest in the country. Females in foster care are six times more likely than teens in the general population to give birth before the age of 21. A new development within the child welfare system is the need to provide accessible, long-term solutions for families as an alternative to removing children from their home.

The important Family Based Services department has created many strategic partnerships with other agencies equally committed to improving the lives of the disenfranchised. St. Anne's, a key provider of services, is a ray of sunshine in the surrounding community.

NEW VILLAGE CHARTER HIGH SCHOOL

McAlister High School, on the St. Anne's campus, was constructed in 1964 and for over 40 years operated as a school for pregnant minors under a lease to Los Angeles Unified School District (LAUSD). The LAUSD lease expired in 2006, and St. Anne's entered into a collaboration with a number of other organizations and community leaders to organize a new charter high school which would become the lessee of the school facility and provide an educational opportunity tailored to the needs of St. Anne's residents and other needy young women.

New Village Charter High School

The new school, New Village Charter School, was chartered by LAUSD and organized as a non-profit public benefit corporation under California law. By action of the California State Board of Education, New Village was authorized to operate as a single-gender school for girls; it is the only single-gender charter school in California. New Village has its own Board of Directors and is legally, financially and organizationally separate from St. Anne's. However, St. Anne's has the right to designate one-third of the New Village directors, and staff of the two organizations have worked closely together on the school program and services. Most St. Anne's residents in 2007 attend New Village, and babies and toddlers of many New Village students from the Rampart neighborhood are enrolled in St. Anne's Early Education Center along with children of St. Anne's residents and other families in the neighborhood.

New Village seeks to provide a rich and relevant college-preparatory curriculum, of a quality comparable to Southern California's finest private, charter and magnet schools, for a student body that includes young women who face extraordinary educational challenges as the result of foster care and probation placements, disruptive family histories, extreme poverty, abuse, neglect and early pregnancy and motherhood, as well as girls from the community who seek an outstanding education in a small school environment. New Village opened with 9th and 10th grades for its first school year. In 2007, 11th grade was added; and 12th grade will be added in 2008. At full capacity, New Village will have between 200 and 240 students, of whom approximately one-fourth are expected to be St. Anne's residents and the remainder are expected to come from the community.[69]

St. Anne's is building brighter futures [70]

As we enter the next 100 years of service to the Los Angeles community, we are all truly amazed by the extraordinary work so many have done before us. St. Anne's has become a Los Angeles landmark, which for many has served as a crucial connection to their past and to their future.

We now enter a new stage. Based on the work completed by 2007, St. Anne's Board of Directors completed a plan that helped set the direction for the next five years. These decisions were not created in a vacuum—they were the results of extensive interviews with key stakeholders including our board members, trustees, referring agencies, collaborative partners, staff and, most important, the young women we serve. They have told us they wish to remain connected to St. Anne's, their fear of having no home to live in, no care for their children, and no one to feel connected to.

Learning that, the St. Anne's board had decided to create more housing in the communities around St. Anne's and additional child care to support them. This will be permanent housing that will allow these young women to keep the apartment in the future, to pay the full rent, to have a home.

What else would those who have committed themselves to this mission do but to step forward to meet such a critical need?

So, as you read this book and learn the history of this remarkable agency, look ahead to the future. That is where St. Anne's is going. We hope you will join us.

From a small 12-bed facility in 1908, St. Anne's looks to the future in 2008 after a century of service extending to the next century a

LEGACY OF LOVE

Notes

THE FIRST ST. ANNE'S: FIFTEENTH & FIGUEROA—1908[71]

There is every reason to be proud of the efforts made today in every community for the people who care for all classes of sick people. The science of the physician has combined with the skill of the nurse to give the sick all the advantages of education (as well as human sympathy). In the care of the sick, the Catholic Church has always recognized not only the skill of the physicians but also the power of God to bestow the strength of life and renewed health as a reward for the earnest prayer of the people.

The new hospital building is a private residence in the mission style. It was built but a few years ago. The first floor contains a reception hall, two private rooms for patients, the dining room and the office. On the second floor there are two wards of four beds each, one private room, the delivery room and the nursery. Four beds are provided for charity patients. On the rear of the lot there is a small building (originally an automobile garage) and this has been transformed into a pleasant home for the nurses in charge of the hospital. At the foot of the stairway in the reception hall, a beautiful statue of the Sacred Heart had been placed, the gift of Mrs. Ellen Donohoe of Compton.

ST. ANNE'S LOCATIONS AND NAME CHANGES

Just before Christmas in 1911, St. Anne's moved from its original location at Fifteenth and Figueroa to a newly constructed bungalow called Rosary Villa. Located at 700 East Lomita Avenue in Glendale, the facility was named *St. Anne's Infant Home* and had a capacity for

26 babies. At the time, three infants were in the care of the staff. These three were moved to the new location.

The little Glendale shelter simply was not large enough, so nine months later in 1912, the institution moved into larger quarters, conducting a successful infant's shelter. The facility then moved to 343 West Avenue in Los Angeles, but the location near the Jesuit College proved impractical. Not long after, the operation moved to 4599 Marmion Way in Highland Park. But this move was only to last one year. The name was changed to *St. Anne's Orphanage*. When the number of children reached fifteen, larger quarters were needed.

In November of 1914, the services were moved to Venice and the name was changed to *St. Anne's Infant Asylum*. In her diary, Miss Donnelly noted happily that for the first time, Bishop Conaty granted permission for a chapel as a part of the home.

Apparently in 1915, there were two Hollywood locations, one at 6012 Hollywood Boulevard, the second in August at 6041 Hollywood Boulevard. The name changed to St. Anne's Infant Home. Thirty children were cared for until the age of three when they were sent to the Sisters' Orphans Home in Boyle Heights.

In 1915, Mrs. Katherine Stamps donated a parcel of land and buildings located at 1044 North Mariposa Street, to the St. Vincent de Paul Society. Occasional improvements were made on the property which would prove to be helpful in the years to come.

In 1922, Mrs. Stamps gave the lot adjoining the property on Mariposa to the Diocese of Los Angeles and San Diego. In 1928, a two-story stucco building was purchased by the Diocese and moved onto the lot.

ST. ANNE'S MATERNITY HOSPITAL GUILD

The Guild became incorporated in 1956, making it a non-profit corporation with both the State and Federal tax authorities. The Board of Directors approved the action on April 17th and the incorporation was completed on July 3, 1956.

Initially the Guild was separately incorporated, but in July of 1964, the members decided it would be in their best interest to become an integral part of the St. Anne's Maternity Hospital. In doing so, the Guild benefited from St. Anne's insurance and tax exempt status. Dissolution was completed in a certificate filed with the California Secretary of State on March 19, 1965, which was ratified by the Board of Directors.

DEDICATION OF THE FIRST NEW ADDITION

The new little wing at St. Anne's was dedicated on April 7, 1941. The Right Reverend Msgr. Thomas J. O'Dwyer, Archdiocesan Director of Health and Hospitals, presided. Guests of honor included the Honorable Fletcher Bowron, Mayor of Los Angeles; Charles Fox Stamps, son of the Founders, Mrs. Kate Fox Stamps; Mrs. Marie Campbell, first Superintendent. of St. Anne's; Mrs. Thomas Lewis (Loretta Young); Honorable Joseph Scott; John McDevitt, M.D., President of St. Anne's Medical Staff; Arthur J. Will, President of the Association of California Hospitals; Lynn Mowatt, General Manager of L.A. Community Welfare Federation; Leroy Bruce, Director of L.A. General Hospital; John M. Zuck, Chief Probation Officer of L.A. County, M. L. Barker and Lawrence Ott, Architects; and J. E. and T. J. Haddock, General Contractors. Approximately four hundred guests gathered in the patio in front of the main entrance of the hospital.

ST. ANNE'S FOUNDATION

The Archdiocese was in favor of the concept of the Foundation although there was no direct financial support. On the support of the Foundation from the Archdiocese, Most Reverend Joseph T. McGucken said:

It would be a good thing to set up a foundation. If the foundation exists it would naturally attract donations, whereas if it has no official existence, people might look elsewhere to place their funds. If such cooperation were founded, I think it would be best to have your own corporation and further, it would be desirable to have the officers of the corporation as the officers of the Queen of Angels Hospital. These officers would be the Trustees of the Corporation. In addition to the Trustees, I would think there should be an advisory board, which would include lay people, who would help to further the interests of the foundation.[72]

Charter Members of the Foundation[73]

First Trustees of the Foundation
*Sister Mary Winifred Falker
*Sister M. Febronia Maier
Sister M. Hedwig Muller
Sister M. Amabilis Weitzel
Sister M. Ehtelburga Herman
Sister M. Junilla Haskell
Sister M. Theodora Wessel
Joseph Scott
*Mrs. George L. Humphreys
*Thomas H.A. Lewis
*Leo T. McMahon
Mrs. Walter Luer
Kathleen R. Harrington, M.D.
Mrs. Thomas Brant
*Sister M. Madeline Williams
*Sister M. Borromea Feier
Sister M. Siena Mersch
*Sister M. Thomasine McKinnon
Thomas A.J. Dockweiler
Katherine Stearne Dockweiler
Mildred Holleran

Walter M. Holleran
Mrs. Charles Von Der Ahe
Marguerite Winston
George L. Humphreys
Mrs. Cornelius S. Sullivan
Dorothy Clune Murray
Mrs. Randolph Ingersoll
Mrs. Walter P. Story
Mrs. Jerome Hanrahan
Thomas J. O'Neill
*Cora W. Strub
Gladys C. Burns
*Fritz B. Burns
*J. Howard Zieman

HOLY FAMILY ADOPTION SERVICE

Conversations with Archbishop McIntyre indicated that the establishment of an adoption agency would be under the operation of the hospital or the Foundation. The Catholic Welfare Bureau would be represented on the Board of the group operating the agency and would provide guidance and cooperation.[74]

The Foundation's Board of Trustees was very enthusiastic in support of the establishment of the agency.[75] The medical staff strongly supported and believed that a Catholic adoption agency was a pressing need. Some resistance, however, came from the State Department of Social Welfare, which indicated they would only license one Catholic agency in the adoption field for all time.[76] This remained the case for several years although the rationale for this position is undocumented.

Archbishop McIntyre was heartily in favor of the agency.

The splendid work of St. Anne's Maternity Hospital and its correlative—the Holy Family Adoption Service—have an appeal all their own. These works are the expressions of true charity to a "neighbor in need." They involve love in its incipience and the response of human kindness is always warm to the newborn. I am hopeful therefore, that the proposed Bulletin telling of the works of your organization will serve a fruitful purpose and be a medium of many blessings to your generous benefactors.[77]

The Planning Conference on Adoption and Child Care Services convened in San Francisco on September 26th. The conference was stirred into action because of sincere differences of opinion on the adoption bills introduced in the California legislature in 1949 because 85% of the adoptions in the state were done through intermediaries, and were not in a position to protect the interests of children.

Los Angeles County already was aware of the need of these differences. The Citizen's Adoption Committee reported that there were 1,374 independent adoptions in the County of Los Angeles during the 1949-50 year. There were only 145 social agency adoptions and 36.7% of all adoptions were taking place in Los Angeles out of the 58 counties in the state.[78]

Results of the Planning Conference on Adoption and its study: "Initial conclusions of the study undertaken were that adoption is only one method of treatment in a total child care program and the need and value of this depends on the natural family, its strength and adequacy and extent of public and private family agency services, medical child guidance and child care services. It was apparent that these services are entirely inadequate in Los Angeles County. "Adoption," the committee concluded, "must be viewed not as the largest and most luminous planet in our sky, but as a star in a constellation— a star which reflects light that is only clear when the other stars in the constellation—family service, child care, child guidance and medical care—are strong and bright. In part, the Holy Family Adoption Agency in part helped to overcome this problem."[79]

The agency experienced some difficulties, including financial struggles. Attention was given to understanding the unsettled condition of the adoption relationships in California at the time, including the attitude of the legislators on this subject. An administrative consultant, on loan from the Catholic Home Bureau for Dependent Children of New York City, Miss Mary Murray, assisted the agency with reorganization efforts.[80]

A View of Adoption Services in the 1950's

In Los Angeles and elsewhere, there was a concern about the practices of some adoption agencies in what practically could be termed a "mail order" basis. For example, the agency might write a letter to prospective adoptive parents, telling them that they have the "golden haired baby" for them when actually there was no baby at all. The going rate for an adoption in this era was $500 plus an additional $10 for each interview with their social service worker. There was a push to have the adoptions proceed with great haste.

Typically, there were many more applicants than there were babies available for adoption and prospective adoptive parents had to wait at least a year. At the Catholic Welfare Bureau, the approval of a case was completed in about three to five weeks. Local officials seriously interested in promoting correct adoption procedures, felt that releasing the infants should not be done too quickly in order to allow a better knowledge of the infant so that placement is more appropriate. One older agency wrote to the Catholic Welfare Bureau about Holy Family Adoption Service, quite spontaneously congratulating them on the efficiency of their service.[81]

The adoption committee addressed unwed motherhood, which they recognized as a challenge, and a real community problem. Coupled with the rapid change in social values and the breakdown of traditional moral codes, there was direct influence on the unmarried mother to be recognized as one of society's most complicated social and human problems. The adoption committee went a step further when it forged the link between the unmarried mother and problems surrounding the adoption of children.

A nationally prominent physician in the field of hospital administration, Dr. Anthony J.J. Rourke of Stanford University Hospital (and member of the Adoption Committee) stated:

> Look at the funds and facilities that are available to help patients with physical ills, even those in the hopeless stage, and then contrast that to the funds and facilities available to the unwed mother. Look at our attitude toward the child of the unmarried mother…. Unwed mothers are looked on as unfit, immoral, and looked down upon with scorn. We need someone to act the part of the Good Samaritan and come to the rescue of these girls needing help, and remove the cloak which hides the community's responsibility toward these helpless women. We must face the problem of the unwed mother squarely for what it is—a problem of society for which we must all accept a measure of responsibility—a problem that calls for a skillful, humane approach that is based on understanding, and has as its goal, the rehabilitation of its innocent victims.[82]

The scope and size of unmarried motherhood indicated that it is no small problem. In 1947 there were 1,131,900 registered out-of-wedlock live births in the United States, a 50% increase in ten years. The unmarried mother frequently lacks understanding and sympathy from friends, family or the father of the baby. They come from all walks of life. The Citizens Committee is leading the campaign of community understanding to develop informed public opinion in order to maintain the financial assistance now provided to her as caretaker of her unborn child under the present Aid to Needy Children program. The Committee believes that the welfare of the unmarried mother is at stake but that the child has first claim on society for the right to be born a healthy, normal individual.

In 1952, a practice of predatory forces lived on the misfortunes of the unwed mother. An advertisement might say "Lodging and meals given any unwed mother in exchange for light housekeeping." This played on the unwed mother's emotions and in this arrangement she is coerced into giving the baby up for adoption.[83]

The Holy Family Adoption Service initiated an Auxiliary in Long Beach. It was thought that one of the ways to rescue people from dealing in the "black market" of babies was to make potential adoptive parents aware of legitimate agencies set up to find homes for children. Its work would be "interpretive," bringing to the general public an awareness of the agency and the work being done.

The adoption service grew. One distinctive feature of Holy Family Adoption Service was the early placement of babies. It was the agency that was convinced that the baby without affection is a starved baby. Placing the child in the affectionate arms of its adoptive parents must be accomplished at the earliest possible date. Love and affection provided to the child as early as possible has a tremendous impact on the development of the child.

This fact was also included in excerpts included in the newsletter from an article from *TIME Magazine,* May 5, 1952 by Dr. Rene A. Spitz, on the issue of love and affection by parents.[84]

After four years of existence, Holy Family Adoption Agency placed its 300th child into adoption. The first 100 babies were in 22 months, the next 100 occurred in 12 months, and the third 100 happened in 8.5 months. Authorities unanimously declared that this record showed efficiency and growth, and important work of the agency. This was the only agency known to be operating in the eleven Western states which did not charge fees for its services. Several fundraisers were initiated, like the family festival that raised the needed funds to help offset the costs.[85]

When the buildings that once housed Holy Family Adoption Service were demolished in 1968, the agency moved to Westlake. The Los Angeles headquarters were moved once again in 1987 when they relocated to St. Anne's campus to promote adoption as an option for the young girls at St. Anne's. In approximately 1997, the agency moved out of St. Anne's to Pasadena and then in June 2007 moved to Echo Park. With over a half of a century, Holy Family Adoption Agency continued to provide adoptive services in Southern California.

ST. ANNE'S IN THE 1950'S
In 1952, a total of 403 girls were provided services within the following age categories:[86]

Age Range	Number of Girls
12-15	17
16	30
17	25
18	42
19	39
20	28
21	37
22	44
23	32
24	21
25	11
26	6
27	12
28	15
29-42+	44

1955 Expansion

By 1955, the hospital was bursting at the seams. Significant expansion of St. Anne's occurred in 1954-1955 with a new wing, which took shape despite many problems and endless delays. The hospital capacity was lowered during construction and everyone awaited the "move date." In August 1955, even though workmen were still on the premises and the construction was not quite finished, the Sisters began moving residents into the dormitory unit.

The new wing was dedicated on September 11th; a new wing housing 59 prenatal beds, 21 hospital beds and 22 bassinets was dedicated. The 102 bed facility was funded entirely through the support of St. Anne's Hospital Guild and St. Anne's Foundation. The new wing provided additional facilities for the care of 65 girls and 35 babies. Framed cottages were acquired which increased the capacity to an average of 75 to 80 girls. This served St. Anne's well for the next thirty years.[87]

1956

As included in Sister Winifred's annual report to the Guild in 1957, the 1956 racial mix of girls included:

> 411 white; 78 Mexican; 26 Negro; 2 Filipino; 6 Indian; 3 Japanese; 2 Hawaiian. Also included, there were: 474 single; 25 married; 20 divorced; 7 separated, and 2 were widows. This report summarizes our growth through the years.[88]

1957 "Snapshot" of St. Anne's Maternity Hospital

The Newsletter gave a glimpse of the physicians and the Franciscan Sisters serving in the ministry:[89]

Sister M. Justina, Sister Superior
Sister Mary Winifred, Administrator

Sister M. Rose Marie, Controller
Sister M. Stanislaus, Office Manager
Sister M. Borromeo, Housekeeper
Sister M. Sienna, Supervisor, Food Department
Sister M. Carmelita, Nursery Supervisor
Sister M. Rose Blanche, Hospital Supervisor
Sister M. Gaudentia, Laundry Supervisor
Sister M. Charlene, Case Worker
Sister M. Glorianne, House Mother

Honorary Staff
S.J. Becka, MD
Walter M. Holleran, MD
John J. McDevitt, MD
A.H. Parmalee, Sr., MD

Active Staff
James E. Kelly, MD, Chief of Staff
John G. Thom, MD, Vice President
Elmer L. Crehan, MD, Secretary
Ralph Bookman, MD
Chester P. Bonoff, MD
William G. Caldwell, MD
Kathleen Harrington, MD
Robert F. Kelly, MD
M.H. Martin, MD
A.M. McCarthy, MD
Walter J. Nowers, MD
Thomas J. O'Neill, MD
Venustiano Pulido, MD
John T. Ragan, MD
Stephan B. van Adelsberg, MD

Clyde V. Von der Ahe, MD
Edwin B. Whiting, MD

Consulting Staff
A.R. Camero, MD
J.A. Haenel, MD
Earl W. Henry, MD
J. Norman O'Neill, MD
A.H. Parmalee, Jr., MD
Homer C. Pheasant, MD
George Piness, MD
James F. Regan, MD
Robert L. Watson, MD

Dental Staff
Walter O. Gager, DDS
Virgil K. Rollins, DDS
Randolph L. Whaley, DDS

Resident Staff
Richard Goldman, MD
David McAninch, MD
Claire McGann, MD
R.E. Stellar, MD
John W. Bisenius, MD
Chester P. Bonoff, MD
Ralph Bookman, MD

Clinical Research
Sandoz Pharmaceutical Co. of Switzerland provided one of the grants. This international company is one of the largest companies of its kind in the world. The grant was unique in two ways: 1) St. Anne's

was the only known private institution to receive this kind of grant; and 2) the grant contained a fairly liberal application of the funds, determined solely by the Administrator, Sister Mary Winifred. Sandoz published an international journal, *Sandoz Quarterly Cumulative Index*, in which St. Anne's Maternity Hospital was referenced several times for its scope and quality of research. The *Index* was translated into dozens of languages and circulated among research centers and medical schools all over the world. St. Anne's was involved in eight separate studies over a four-year period that focused on conditions during pregnancy such as depression, nausea and vomiting. The importance of the research studies and the international recognition accorded St. Anne's the high standing of the volunteer medical staff.[90]

St. Anne's in the 1960's

Educational Center: In addition to the three classrooms totaling 1,920 square feet, the educational center housed especially designed areas for instruction in arts and crafts, homemaking, music, and a library. Vocational training for girls over 17 years of age also played an important part in the educational center program.

The educational center, designed by H.L. Gogerty, F.A.I.A. of Porter, Gogerty, and Meston, specialists in school and institution architecture, was regarded as a unique laboratory. The 8,400 square-foot one-story structure was completed in just nine months. In most of the areas, an acoustical floor covering had been used for purposes of low maintenance cost, ease in cleaning with soap and water, and the psychological and therapeutic effect upon students and teachers. Window coverings and draw curtains are tub-washable Fiberglas. A Glide-a-Wall installation, invented and patterned by Mr. Gogerty, permitted the main classroom to be divided into 3 separate rooms. The walls were eight-inch blocks, filled with concrete and unpainted to assure low upkeep costs. The roof is bonded for 20 years wearing-quality. Copper piping was used throughout and the under-ground installation had been treated to prevent electrolysis. Lighting is optimum and individual zone air-conditioning units add to the comfort of the occupants. Cabinets were especially designed to give maximum working areas and storage. Much of the movable classroom equipment was supplied to the center by the Los Angeles Board of Education. Landscaping was held to minimal need in the cloistered patio, and lining can be maintained at low cost. Concrete walkways, salt-pitted for safety, are canopy-covered. A public address system that could pipe in FM radio music had been added both for emergency call purposes and security. A fire alarm system with overhead sprinkler valves afforded maximum protection.[91]

1965 Expansion: Expansion of St. Anne's also addressed the problem of separating the administrative work of the hospital from its direct services, streamlining the total agency operation. This provided cohesive integration for its multiple services. In October 1962, a letter was received from the Chancellor of the Archdiocese, Rt. Rev. Msgr. Benjamin G. Hawkes; he wrote that Cardinal McIntyre's Board of Consulters had approved St. Anne's Foundation's proposal to build the new 8,400 square foot educational center across the street from the hospital on Glassell Street. The project was approved as an *urgent* social need by His Eminence, the Los Angeles Area Welfare Planning Council, the California State Department of Social Welfare, and by the Los Angeles Board of Education. It was also approved by the Capital Requirements and Agency Supplementary Fund-Raising Committees of United Way, Incorporated of Los Angeles County, of which St. Anne's Maternity Hospital is a charter agency.

Groundbreaking: Bishop John Ward officiated at the groundbreaking ceremonies for the educational center that were held on January 5, 1964. He was assisted by the Right Revered Monsignor Thomas J. O'Dwyer, S.T.B., Archdiocesan director of health and hospitals, and by the Reverend Herbert Patterson, O.F.M., resident chaplain at St. Anne's.

The educational component at St. Anne's has always been a very critical element in her services since nearly 80% of pregnant teenagers nationwide drop out of school. The success rate at St. Anne's is much higher as evidenced by 1963's record year: out of 184 enrolled students, 8 students graduated from high school and 98 completed the market cashiering course.

Dedication: The blessing of the new facility occurred on October 4, 1964 by Bishop Ward. Principal speaker at the well-attended program was Jack P. Crowher, superintendent of the Los Angeles Unified School District (LAUSD).

Fifty-seven students, from the 9th to 12th grades, moved into the new educational center on Monday, October 5, 1964. Thirty-eight students (17 years of age or older) enrolled in the six-week course in market cashiering. Vons's Markets and City Built Fixtures Company provided the cash registers, scales and check out-stands for the course. The center offered classes in homemaking, business education, choral work and cosmetology, music, homemaking and arts and crafts in specially designed classrooms.

GATEWAY HOUSE

This shelter was founded in 1972 by a group of concerned Pomona citizens who saw the need for dignified and affordable housing for young single parents. Over 100 young women lived at Gateway House in its first eleven years of service.

The Board of Gateway House was no longer able to continue its operation and decided to deed the property over to St. Anne's Maternity Home. The Board formed the "Gateway Guild" and this guild joined other St. Anne's volunteer groups to support St. Anne's, with their special emphasis on the Pomona program.

In a report to the Board of Directors dated October 11, 1982, Sister Margaret Anne Floto, said "that Gateway had been a resource for years and girls were regularly placed there from St. Anne's." The Board of Directors accepted the offer of Gateway House on September 11, 1982. Efforts were made to dissolve the Gateway Corporation by the end of their fiscal year, September 30th, which required a waiver from the Attorney General. Since the usual process of dissolution of a non-profit was two months, a waiver was necessary. With the dissolution of the corporation and obtaining the waiver on September 30th, St. Anne's was able to accept the assets and liabilities on October 1st.

QUEENSCARE FAMILY CLINICS

The Franciscan Sisters responded to an urgent plea from Bishop J.J. Cantwell to establish a hospital in Los Angeles. They began serving at the Cope Mansion in 1925 and formally founded Queen of Angels Hospital in 1926. For a time, Queens was the largest privately owned hospital west of the Mississippi. In 1982, the Daughters of Charity of St. Vincent de Paul assumed operation of the hospital for five years following a period of time in which Queens was leased to a for-profit entity. St. Joseph's Corporation was named sole Corporate Member of Queen of Angels under the leadership of Joe Brandlin and Art Barron.

The hospital was damaged in the 1987 earthquake and an opportunity for merger with Hollywood Presbyterian Medical Center (HPMC) became possible in 1989 and operations were moved from the historic site to HPMC. The clinic (operated by the Sisters) had moved to St. Anne's campus, but to strengthen its financial viability, the Sisters asked QA-HPMC, who operated other local primary care clinics, to take over the operation of the Sisters' clinic. In 1995, the Franciscan Clinic came under the auspices of QA-HPMC. When QA-HPMC was sold in 1998, QueensCare emerged as the name of the new charity.[92]

VILLA MAJELLA

Many of the early pioneers of Villa Majella project served on the Regional Board of Consulters, which was organized to advise and recommend to St. Anne's Board of Directors issues involving the Santa Barbara program. Some of those pioneers were: Mary Klink, Mercedes Roux, Frances (Franny) Morehart (member of St. Anne's Guild), Mary Turtle, and Mary Craig.

The facility enjoyed a fine reputation as a quality care facility rendering care to young women in need, 18 and older. Approximately 22 women annually benefited each year from the services and programs offered, thanks to a handful of caring people who wanted to make a difference in their community.

At Villa Majella, the young women learn about the changes that pregnancy brings; how to manage a budget and household; care for their babies; and to begin or continue an education/career path. Each resident must attend school, work, or serve as a community volunteer during her stay at Villa Majella. Weekly seminars include timely topics such as nutrition, legal rights, coping skills, postpartum depression, adoption/parenting realities, and career opportunities.

By 2007, Villa Majella was still serving pregnant women in need.

FRITZ & GLADYS BURNS WING

Building Features: There was a reduced census in the residential portion, and administrative functions were located there as construction began. The new 81,000 square foot residential center was designed to offer closer supervision of and attention to residents by Child Care Workers. The building was planned with enhanced security and control, offering study areas in each bedroom to accommodate St. Anne's emphasis on education. There were open visiting areas and special rooms for individual and group counseling or private visits and a child care center (i.e., the CDC).

Dedication—February 13, 1992: Bishop John J. Ward, Auxiliary Bishop of Los Angeles, officiated at the ceremony. KABC News Anchorwoman, Ann Martin served as MC. Salam Al Marayati, Director, Muslim Public Affairs Council; Rev. John Bruno, Rector of St.

Athanasius & St. Paul Episcopal Church; Elder James Z. Jacobson, Church of Jesus Christ of Latter-day Saints; Pastor Thomas Kilgore, Jr., Pastor Emeritus, Los Angeles Second Baptist Church; and Rabbi Alfred Wolf, Director, Skirball Institute on American Values extended ecumenical greetings. Sister Mary Mark Segvich, Vicaress of the Franciscan Sisters of the Sacred Heart and Evelyn Blasiar, President of St. Anne's Foundation, Sister Margaret Anne Floto, Chairman of the Board and Tom Owenson, Executive Director of St. Anne's, also addressed the well-wishers on hand to celebrate this exciting moment in St. Anne's history.

RESIDENTIAL EDUCATION AND TREATMENT

A behavioral-level system is a typical feature of group homes. This structure allowed the residents to earn privileges by following house rules and taking personal responsibility. At the heart of the facility, the residential counselors act as mothers and fathers to the residents, helping the girls work out interpersonal problems that stem from their pasts fraught with physical, substance, sexual abuse, and emotional neglect.

Along with this comprehensive education package, the residential program offered vocational assistance and recreational/social activities for at-risk pregnant and parenting teen girls (ages 11 to 18) and their children (birth to age 3) who came to St. Anne's. A full schedule of ten-week courses was tailored to the residents' particular needs. Core courses complemented students' regular academic work. Some of the elective courses included first aid, "mommy & me," cooking, "sound beginnings," and psychodrama. An improved education program integrated the learning center with computers featuring typing, math, resume writing, and English tutorial software. Accredited teachers assisted the residents to become computer-literate. The whole program focused on developing the individual's strength and helped to create constructive solutions that directed these young people to more productive and healthy lifestyles.

Educational and vocational training are a priority at St. Anne's but it is challenging to locate records from other institutions where residents have been placed. Staff members work small miracles to obtain necessary school records and find appropriate school placements for residents. Many of our teens had only experienced failure in school, yet St. Anne's staff is able to renew and maintain their efforts to complete school.

The **CDC** gave the young mothers practical experience in rearing a child. It was a place where residents learned in class how to care for their infants. This was the best "hands on" training available. Goals for the mothers included developing and improving parenting skills to eliminate the risk of child abuse along with fostering self-nurturing and coping skills, developing routines, establishing boundaries and strong communication skills. New mothers had to first complete a four-week training program that taught feeding, how to attend to a crying child, or properly change a diaper, and all that comes with an infant or toddler. The staff became positive role models for the young mothers, which showed the residents healthy ways to interact with their children. The staff fostered trust and autonomy by meeting the physical and emotional needs of the infants and toddlers.

Emancipation: A new feature in the residence presented new "emancipation" curricula. The elements of the program assisted residents with extra support as the residents prepared to deal with the realities of independent living. Those selected for emancipation were those who had great success in the residential program. They created and managed their own schedules, arrived at appointments on time; completed chores; worked at outside jobs; did their own food shopping, planned a menu and cooked a meal one day each week, as well as spending quality time with their children. This taught the residents to navigate this important transition to independence; no one did it for them, but helped them target and achieve goals for themselves. The program included 14 emancipation goals which focused on essential independent living skills such as banking, budgeting, nutrition, basics of cooking, resume writing, interview, job searches and other needed skills.

Twelve mothers and their babies were accommodated at one time in this unit. Once a resident had been on campus for at least sixty days and showed some positive progress toward completing her goals, she went through an interview process before being accepted.

Clinical Services: Initially these were provided by licensed social workers who met with the residents in individual and group therapy sessions. They served as liaisons between St. Anne's and various placement agencies, schools, families and the baby's father, if he was involved. To give residents the maximum amount of support, the therapists worked with probation offers and others to create clear and definable limits.

Specialized therapy groups were created for therapeutic support; St. Anne's hosted 12-step groups for Alcoholics Anonymous, and ethnic awareness groups to foster residents' understanding of their ethnic histories, customs and cultures which cultivated better understanding among the residents.

Vocational training: This was another component of the educational program. In 2003, 21 residents were working at in-house and external jobs including Pizza Hut, Smart & Final, the Los Angeles County Law Library, LAUSD, Bank of America and Goodwill. These opportunities helped to build confidence in the residents for future employment situations. The Aviva Skills Center provided computer training skills in various Microsoft applications as well as clerical, cashier and office training. The participants even earned $150 if they completed the program. The Independent Living Program (ILP) focused on life skills, not to mention resume writing, interviewing techniques and job search strategies.

By the year 2000, the residential services were expanded to embrace teenage girls who were neither pregnant nor parenting but who were at risk of becoming so. The staff's expertise in providing a safe, healing, nurturing and learning environment for adolescents was equally needed and effective in helping these abused young women. In 2000, out of the 249 residents, 17 were neither pregnant nor parenting. St. Anne's Outreach program also assisted. It allows the opportunity to provide education aimed at preventing teen pregnancy by empowering young people to resist the pressures in our society, which suggest sexual experimentation as an appropriate adolescent experience.

THE OUTREACH PROGRAM

The Outreach program, launched in 1986, continued into the 1990's and provided "outposts of crucial services delivered directly to pregnant and parenting young people in their home communities." This program was all about prevention and ways to interrupt the dysfunctional cycles within the families that had contributed to the pregnancies. These counselors focused on the promotion of positive life skills that encouraged healthy and healing relationships. Some former residents of St. Anne's needed further guidance and support to prepare them for re-entry into society's mainstream. These young people received services from Outreach as well. The other goal of Outreach was to enhance the public's understanding of the causes and consequences of teen pregnancy.

The expansion of services included Teen Issues Week, a complete prevention and decision-making curriculum where four educators went into a school for up to five days and spoke to every student. Twelve schools invited St. Anne's to conduct such a week. Hundreds of youth also attended two all-day teen conferences, one in the spring and the other in the fall. Presentations to parent groups and teachers were part of the Outreach.

An innovative series, S.T.A.Y.I.N.G. True to Yourself (Students Talking About Youth Issues for the Next Generation) was launched in 1998 by St. Anne's. This peer education program trained young people in a teen issues curriculum that they could then present in their own school and at middle schools. St. Monica's High School in Santa Monica served as the pilot school for the project.

Studies show that people learn best from their own peers, and the same is true of teens. The credibility factor is higher when teens hear other teens talk about goal-setting and abstinence. To recognize that anyone's life can be changed forever with one irresponsible decision, when that message is carried by peers, it tends to stick a whole lot more.[93]

The Outreach is multi-varied and the sheer numbers in 1995 speak for themselves. Almost 1,000 clients received comprehensive case management services and another 340 persons were in weekly support groups. The social workers' logs noted that 570 persons received assistance and referrals, and another 5,412 students and parents attended 55 educational presentations and 400 workshops were given with 9,051 students in attendance.[94]

Education for the general teen population in 1995 offered a "Prevention Conference" about responsible teen sexuality. Elements of the conference included setting goals, developing self-esteem principles and a peer panel who "tells it like it is" about the realities of teen pregnancy. The first conference had 160 parenting teens attending from Los Angeles and Ventura counties. Another conference held on Mother's Day weekend was entitled "There's a Hero Found in You: Guiding Teen Moms Toward Excellence."

In November of 1990, a new job training program was offered at McAlister High School and other district schools which supplement the job training already offered at Metropolitan Skills Center. It was a joint venture between the LAUSD, the City of Los Angeles, the Los Angeles Private Industry Council and Big Sisters of Los Angeles. This kickoff of the new program even warranted a visit from Mayor Tom Bradley and Los Angeles School Superintendent, Leonard Britton, to kick it off. Curriculum included job training, entry employment experience along with special prenatal instruction, physical fitness programs and parenting classes as well as basic skills education. Because about 20% of teen mothers drop out of school, it emphasizes the importance of a program like this so that they can obtain the skills they need for a well-paying job.[95]

There have been positive results to St. Anne's premium on education as it has played a major role in helping the residents realize their potential and true ability. The statistics themselves are impressive. The residents are more likely to:

65%   Graduate from high school
50%   More likely to be working
48%   Less likely to be on welfare than their pregnant/parenting
       peers

Since McAlister opened its doors in 1964, approximately 10,000 young women have taken advantage of the educational opportunities there. St. Anne's is more than brick and mortar; at the heart of what we do is the compassionate care. "The purpose of the building is service. We are here to serve those who come to us, desperately in need of what we can provide."[96]

References

Part One

1. Falker, Sister Winifred, "Remarks-Tea & Talk," October 24, 1962.

2. St. Anne's, *Angel Messenger Newsletter,* "65th Anniversary Edition," 1973.

3. *The Tidings,* Los Angeles, CA, "Dedication of St. Anne's Maternity Hospital," November 6, 1908.

4. *The Tidings,* Los Angeles, CA, "Dedication of St. Anne's Maternity Hospital," November 6, 1908.

5. One reference stated that another name for the facility was "St. Vincent Maternity Hospital and Saint Anne Infant Home" See: Weber, Msgr. Francis J., Archivist, Archdiocese of Los Angeles. *A Legacy of Healing: The Story of Catholic Health Care in the Archdiocese of Los Angeles.* Mission Hills, California: Saint Francis Historical Society, 2003, page 70. The Home was not to be confused with the larger St. Vincent's Hospital conducted by the Daughters of Charity of St. Vincent de Paul. The only connection between the two was Dr. Malony (the first physician to serve at St. Anne's) was on the staff of the two hospitals: St. Vincent's and Queen of Angels as well as another hospital located on Figueroa.

6. St. Anne's Brochure preserved in Archives at the Motherhouse of the Franciscan Sisters of the Sacred Heart, Frankfort, Illinois.

7. Keyes, Francis Parkinson, *St. Anne—Grandmother of Our Saviour* (New York: Hawthorn Books, Inc., 1955).

8. St. Anne's Guild, "History of St. Anne's Guild," booklet, 1938-1958.

Part Two

9. Ibid, Falker, 1962.

10. Ibid, Falker, 1962.

11. Ibid, Falker, 1962.

12. McGucken, Joseph T., Auxiliary Bishop of Los Angeles, "To Sister Mary Winifred," letter, July 6, 1945.

13. Ibid, Falker, 1962.

14. St. Anne's Foundation, "The Gracious Story of St. Anne's," booklet, circa 1941.

15. Articles of Incorporation, St. Anne's Foundation.

16. Notes taken from undated brochure, St. Anne's, "Regardless of society's attitude toward the unwed mother, no one wants to brand any child with a social stigma. To safeguard the child, St. Anne's protects the mother; quiets her fears; and gives her security and protection." Capacity is 36; 40 live outside the hospital until delivery. In 1946, 247 patients were admitted.

17. Newsletter (St. Anne's Foundation, June 1951). Hospital's first newsletter.

18. St. Anne's Board of Directors Meeting, August 7, 1950.

19. Ludlam, J.E. "To J. Francis McIntyre," Telegram, March 28, 1952.

20. The Citizens Committee on Adoption, Circa April 1952.

21. Newsletter (St. Anne's Foundation, August, 1961).

22. Newsletter (St. Anne's Foundation, April 1953).

23. Newsletter (St. Anne's Foundation, May 1953). Author of poem and relationship to St. Anne's not indicated.

24. Newsletter (St. Anne's Foundation, December 1953).

25. Ibid, Falker, 1962.

26. Newsletter (St. Anne's Foundation, August 1957).

27. Newsletter (St. Anne's Foundation, July-August 1956).

28. Ibid (Newsletter, October 1957.) W.H. Masters was from the Department of Obstetrics & Gynecology, Washington University School of Medicine, St. Louis, MO.

29. Falker, Sister Mary Winifred, "St. Anne's Guild Annual Meeting," notes, February 6, 1957. Newsletter (St. Anne's Foundation, September 1956).

30. Newsletter (St. Anne's Foundation, October 1958).

31. Newsletter (St. Anne's Foundation, July-August, 1958). Cited article from *Newsweek,* June 30, 1958.

32. Newsletter (St. Anne's Foundation, October 1958).

33. Ibid, Newsletter, October 1958.

34. Newsletter (St. Anne's Foundation, September-October 1989).

35. Newsletter (St. Anne's Foundation, May 1962).

36. Newsletter (St. Anne's Foundation, September 1962).

37. Newsletter (St. Anne's Foundation, Summer 1961).

38. Newsletter (St. Anne's Foundation, Summer 1963).

39. Newsletter (St. Anne's Foundation, June 1964).

40. Newsletter (St. Anne's Foundation, August 1968).

41. Ibid, Newsletter, 1968.

42. Guswiler, Mert, *Herald Examiner,* July 26, 1970.

43. *Angel Messenger,* (St. Anne's, 1970, Vol 4, #3).

PART THREE

44. *Angel Messenger,* (St. Anne's, Summer 1974).

45. *Angel Messenger,* (St. Anne's, March-April 1977).

46. *Angel Messenger,* (St. Anne's, July-August 1980).

47. Ibid, *Angel Messenger* 1980.

48. *Angel Messenger,* (St. Anne's, February 1978).

49. Ibid, February 1978.

50. St. Anne's Annual Report, 1987.

51. *Angel Messenger,* (St. Anne's, September-October 1990).

52. St. Anne's Annual Report, 1988.

53. St. Anne's Annual Report, 1993.

54. *Angel Messenger,* (St. Anne's, Winter 1999).

55. St. Anne's Annual Report, 2001.

56. Lesher, David, "State of the State," *Los Angeles Times,* January 30, 1996, Part A, Page 1.

57. *Angel Messenger,* (St. Anne's, Winter 1998) Quote by Gunther, Steve, Vice President, Programs.

58. St. Anne's, "Capital Campaign Brochure," Circa 1990.

59. St. Anne's Annual Report, 2000.

60. *Angel Messenger,* (St. Anne's, Fall 2004).

61. *Angel Messenger,* (St. Anne's, Winter 2001).

62. *Angel Messenger,* (St. Anne's, Fall 2004).

63. St. Anne's Annual Report, 1997.

64. *Angel Messenger,* (St. Anne's, Winter 2005).

65. *Angel Messenger,* (St. Anne's, Spring 2007).

66. Ibid, *Angel Messenger,* Spring 2007.

67. *Angel Messenger,* (St. Anne's, Fall 2006).

68. St. Anne's, "Family Based Services," Program Description.

69. *Angel Messenger,* (St. Anne's, Fall 2006)

70. Contributed by Tony Walker, MA, St. Anne's President and CEO.

NOTES

71. Ibid, *Tidings,* 1908.

72. McGucken, Joseph T., Auxiliary Bishop of Los Angeles to Sister Mary Winfred, (letter, July 6, 1945).

73. St. Anne's Articles of Incorporation—1946.

74. McIntyre, Archbishop Francis to Sister Mary Winifred, (memo, April 29, 1949).

75. Lewis, Loretta Young, President of St. Anne's Foundation to Most Reverend J. Francis McIntyre, Archbishop of Los Angeles, (letter, March 4, 1949).

76. Falker, Sister Mary Winifred to Archbishop James Francis McIntyre, (memo, 1949).

77. Ibid, Newsletter, June 1951.

78. Citizen's Adoption Committee of Los Angeles, (report, June 28, 1951).

79. Ibid, Citizen's Committee, 1951.

80. St. Anne's Board of Directors (meeting minutes, August 7, 1950).

81. McGucken, Joseph T., Auxiliary Bishop of Los Angeles, Vicar General to Sister Mary Winifred Falker, (letter, February 2, 1949).

82. Ibid, Citizen's Committee, 1951.

83. Newsletter (St. Anne's Foundation, April 1953).

84. Newsletter (St. Anne's Foundation, June 1952), referenced article from *Time Magazine,* May 5, 1952

85. Newsletter (St. Anne's Foundation, August 1953).

86. Newsletter (St. Anne's Foundation, December 1953).

87. Sister Mary Winifred, (St. Anne's report, February 10, 1978).

88. Falker, Sister Mary Winifred, (St. Anne's Guild Annual Meeting, report, February 6, 1957).

89. Newsletter (St. Anne's Foundation, July-August 1957).

90. Newsletter (St. Anne's Foundation, October 1959).

91. Newsletter (St. Anne's Foundation, November 1964).

92. St. Joseph's Health Support Alliance (brochure, "Over 100 Years of Service to Those In Need" 2005).

93. St. Anne's Annual Report, 1999.

94. St. Anne's Annual Report, 1995.

95. *Angel Messenger* (St. Anne's, January-February 1990).

96. St. Anne's Annual Report, 1990.

The People of St. Anne's

St. Anne's Board of Directors
2007-2008

Andrew E. Bogen — Chairman

*Sister Christine Bowman, O.S.F. — Co-Vice Chair

Michael Scott Feeley — Co-Vice Chair

Allyson B. Simpson — Secretary

Javier Jay Guerena — Treasurer

David A. Abel

Dolores Bononi

*Yolanda S. Brown

*Scott Campbell

*Ruth Charles

Martha Corbett

*Joyce Dinel

*Janet Feeley

David A. Fuhrman

George Gibbs, Jr.

Lynne M. Hook

Katharine K. Hughes

William T. Huston

Sister Norma Janssen, O.S.F.

Robert D. Kerslake

*Richard M. Lizdenis

Brian W. Matthews

Lynne Norwick

*Patrick Pascal

*Dale Pelch

Ronald Preissman

Donald J. Pfaff
John J. Rangel
Victoria Richards
Vincent W. Thorpe
Joyce Walter
Jennifer Woodard

TRUSTEES FOR LIFE
Paul D. Berman
Janette H. Flintoft

HONORARY TRUSTEES
Thomas Hammer
Marye Kimoto
David Oakley

GUILD AND AUXILIARY PRESIDENTS
Dolores Bononi
Guild
Mrs. Kathy Koch-Weser
St. Anne's Junior Guild
Pat Castranova
Sister Winifred Auxiliary
Denise Reiser
Loretta Young Auxiliary
Mrs. Emmanuel Vourgourakis (Mary)
Mabel Mosler Auxiliary

ST. ANNE'S GUILD — PAST PRESIDENTS

Mrs. George L. Humphreys, Founder	1938-1945
Mrs. Fritz B. Burns	1946-1947, 1957
Mrs. Byron Ferris Story	1948-1949
Mrs. Henry L. Clark	1950-1951

Mrs. John B. Rauen	1952-1953
Mrs. J. Norman O'Neill	1954-1955
Mrs. Edmund F. Schnieders	1956
Miss Eileen Keliher Jeffers	1958
Mrs. Ralph D. Sweeney	1959
Mrs. Earl J. Bannon	1960
Mrs. John Francis Roney	1961
Mrs. Eugene Patrick Fay	1962-1963
Mrs. James H. Stell	1964-1965
Mrs. Edward R. Winchell	1966
Mrs. Dolores Lorang Martin	1967-1968
Mrs. Richard W. Bland	1969-1970
Mrs. Clifford R. Anderson, Jr.	1971
Mrs. Victor Charles Winnek	1972-1973
Mrs. Jack Evans	1974-1975
Mrs. John J. Meichtry	1976-1977
Mrs. Arthur M. Reilly	1978, 1981-1982
Mrs. Robert E. Byrne	1979-1980
Mrs. William J. Scully	1983-1984
Mrs. Maurice E. Harrison, Jr.	1985-1986
Mrs. Nick M. Mancinelli	1987
Mrs. Herman J. Hunter	1988-1989
Mrs. Kenneth M. Reid	1990
Mrs. Ronald A. Bononi	1991-1993, 2007
Mrs. John L. Cecil	1993-1994
Mrs. W. Michael Chambers	1994-1996, 2004
Mrs. Una Devlin Lynch	1996-1998
Mrs. Mark Montgomery	1998-2000
Mrs. Richard P. Byrne	2001-2003
Mrs. Irene Miernyk	2005-2006

St. Anne's Angel Award Recipients

1982

Mrs. Ronald Reagan

Mrs. Gladys Carson Burns

1984

Miss Loretta Young

Mr. Art Linkletter

1986

Mrs. Joan Leslie Caldwell

Mr. Lawrence Welk

1988

Mrs. Ann Blyth McNulty

Mr. Henry Gogerty, FAIA

1990

Mrs. Rosemary Cassidy Berman

1991

Mrs. Evelyn Blasair

1992

Mrs. Mary Byrne

1993

Mrs. Marion Driver Carr

1994

Mrs. Catherine Winnek

1995

Mrs. Frances Morehart

1996

Mrs. Rosemary Marco

1997

Honorable John Ferraro

1998

Mr. William T. Huston

Mrs. Dolores Bononi

1999

Doctor Clyde Von der Ahe

Mrs. Kenneth Reid

Mr. Andrew E. Bogen

2000

Mr. Frederick Ruopp

2001

Mrs. Caroline Leonetti Ahmanson

2002

Mr. Tom Owenson

2003

Ms. Linda Alvarez

Ms. Adrienne Medawar

2004

Mr. Rocky Delgadillo

2005

Mr. Michael Novarese

Mr. Robert Nelson

Kenneth & Joyce Skinner

2006

Patricia Brown

Joan Payden

2007

Ruth Charles

David Fuhrman

Special Volunteer Recognition

Mary Byrne

2008

Franciscan Sisters of the Sacred Heart

St. Anne's Guilds and Auxiliaries

Katharine & Roger Hughes

St. Anne's Foundation
Established July 30, 1946

Past Presidents

Mrs. George L. Humphreys

Mrs. Loretta Young Lewis

Mrs. Fritz B. Burns

Mrs. Henry L. Clark

Charles J. Dunn

Hon. Arthur S. Guerin

George Piness, M.D.

Walter R. Von der Ahe

Mrs. Henry G. Mosler

William R. Howell

Jess E. Benton

Alan R. Woodard

Robert F. Gooch

Mrs. Henry M. Berman

F. Parker Geesen

Hon. Kathleen Parker

C. Richard Sprigs

Mrs. Richard Bland

Kenneth Reid

Paul Berman

Donald Pfaff

Mrs. C. Dusty Blasiar

William Witt

Javier Guerena

Janette Flintoft

Lynne Norwick

Janet Feeley

Scott Campbell

PAST CHAIRPERSONS — BOARD OF DIRECTORS

Mother M. Johanna Reiplinger	1941-1948
Mother M. Ursulina Greider	1948-1957
Mother M. Adeline Mazure	1957-1963
Mother Timothy Marie Flaherty	1963-1974
Mother M. Edwardine Ley	1974-1979
Sister Theresa Ettelbrick	1979-1980
Sister Margaret Anne Floto	1980-1997
Mr. Andrew Bogen	1997 to present

FRANCISCAN SISTERS OF THE SACRED HEART ASSIGNED TO ST. ANNE'S

Sister M. Sister M. Agnes Kulas, OSF

Sister M. Anthony Clare Floto, OSF

Sister M. Bede Hogg, OSF

Sister M. Borromea Feier, OSF

Sister Bridget Mary Brett, OSF

Sister M. Carmelita Dominguez, OSF

Sister M. Charlene Schweickert, OSF

Sister Christine Bowman, OSF

Sister Clara Marie Dietz, OSF

Sister M. Clare Van Vooren, OSF

Sister M. Clotilde Barcomb, OSF

Sister M. Doris Mudore, OSF

Sister M. Dorothy Klingelhoet, OSF

Sister M. Fabiola Schaefer, OSF

Sister M. Gaudentia Reuter, OSF

Sister M. Glorianne Leone, OSF

Sister M. Guadalupe De La O, OSF

Sister M. Huberta Forst, OSF

Sister M. Joanita Grochowski, OSF

Sister M. Justina Gartner, OSF

Sister M. Kelly Ann Armstrong, OSF
Sister M. Luella Polaitis, OSF
Sister M. Luitgardis Totzki, OSF
Sister M. Madeleine Williams, OSF
Sister M. Magna Wylepski, OSF
Sister M. Margaret Anne Floto, OSF
Sister M. Marie Meyer, OSF
Sister Mariella Millier, OSF
Sister M. Marina Scholl, OSF
Sister Mary Blanche Arendt, OSF
Sister Mary Flora Papesh, OSF
Sister Mary Genevieve Gallaher, OSF
Sister Mary Jane Sola, OSF
Sister Mary Joan Miller, OSF
Sister Mary Terese Lichko, OSF
Sister Mary Winifred Falker, OSF
Sister Melitta Bach, OSF
Sister Miriam Franik, OSF
Sister M. Natalia Wellner, OSF
Sister Norma Jean (Dismas) Janssen, OSF
Sister Pauline Racich, OSF
Sister Robert Marie Barclay, OSF
Sister M. Rosalia Fueglister, OSF
Sister M. Rose Blanche Neil, OSF
Sister M. Siena Mersch, OSF
Sister M. Theresa Marie Romich, OSF
Sister M. Therese Diane (M. Gerard) Lopez, OSF
Sister M. Thomasine McKinnon, OSF
Sister M. Urbana Kappeler, OSF
Mother M. Ursulina Greider, OSF

100TH ANNIVERSARY COMMITTEE

CO-CHAIRPERSONS

Sister Christine Bowman, OSF, and Ronald Preissman

COMMITTEE MEMBERS

Dolores Bononi

Linda Rowley Blue

Yolanda S. Brown

Joan Leslie Caldwell

Tom Owenson

Allyson B. Simpson

Joyce Walter

Carole Tremblay, Events Consultant

STAFF

Tony Walker, M.A., President/CEO

Steve Gunther, Chief Operating Officer

Cathy Galarneau, Vice President, Development

Christine Hardy, Grants and Communications Manager

St. Anne's

155 N. Occidental Blvd.

Los Angeles, CA 90026

Phone: 213-381-2931

Fax: 213-381-7804

http://www.stannes.org

100 Years of Building Brighter Futures

Index

Index

At this point in history we have to think of ourselves as more than social service agencies, we have to think of ourselves as social engineers, literally altering the future of our young people's lives and their children. Social change does not just happen on its own, it takes leadership of the kind which is happening at St. Anne's. There are few agencies either locally or nationally, that compare.

Gisselle Acevedo
President & CEO
Para Los Niños   Los Angeles

When Carol and I moved to Los Angeles some thirty years ago, we learned about the incredible ministry of the Franciscan Sisters and St. Anne's. We were overjoyed with the fact that the Sisters had extended their arms to embrace this social issue with a full heart. Carol and I embrace St. Anne's legacy of love with all the love in our hearts.

Carol & Dom DeLuise
Actor & Author

I first became acquainted with St Anne's through my work with abused women and unwed mothers. This book is a fascinating insight into the history behind the wonderful work of St. Anne's. I applaud those who contributed to telling the story and for the incredible amount of time and love put into the research.

Georgia Durante
Author of *The Company She Keeps*
and Hollywood Stuntwoman

St. Anne's has served women and children in our community for 100 years, and I am proud that it is located in my district. St. Anne's staff and volunteers work everyday to empower people to break the cycle of poverty, abuse, and neglect. I am so proud to have partnered with St. Anne's to provide transitional housing for emancipated young women so that they can go to school and work to improve their futures. Simply put, St. Anne's is the heart of this city and they have helped to give hope and a brighter future to thousands of people.

Eric Garcetti
President, Los Angeles City Council

This is the kind of story that everyone should read. It is an inspiring, motivating narrative and as an "Angel" in 1984, I congratulate everyone connected with St. Anne's.

Art Linkletter – Entertainer

I believe life has hidden gifts in its hands, the greatest being love and hope. St. Anne's gives these gifts every moment of every day. They warm the cold, soothe the hurt, and feed the soul simply because they care enough. The hope they give to pregnant and parenting teens and their children turn ordinary days into miracles. Because they take away the hurt and bring a smile where there was none before, I will always think of them as heroes.

Flavia Weedn